MW00582824

CLIMB HIGH, CLIMB FAR

Inspiration for Life's Challenges from the World's Great Moral Traditions

GREGORY AND SUZANNE M. WOLFE

A Fireside Book Published by Simon & Schuster

FIRESIDE
Rockefeller Center
1230 Avenue of the Americas
New York, NY 10020

FIRESIDE and colophon are registered trademarks
of Simon & Schuster Inc.

Designed by Chris Welch

Manufactured in the United States of America

1   3   5   7   9   10   8   6   4   2

Library of Congress Cataloging-in-Publication Data

Wolfe, Gregory.
Climb high, climb far : inspiration for life's challenges from the
world's great moral traditions / Gregory and Suzanne M. Wolfe.
        p.   cm.
1. Conduct of life.   I. Wolfe, Suzanne M.   II. Title.
            BJ1581.2.W625   1997
170'.44—dc20   96-30177
                        CIP

ISBN 0-684-80112-4

FOR KATHRYN
AND
IN MEMORY OF JOHN MCENTEE

Climb high
Climb far
Your goal the sky
Your aim the star.

Anonymous, from an inscription on
Hopkins Memorial Steps,
Williams College, Williamstown, Massachusetts

Acknowledgments

This book was originally conceived by Mitch Horowitz, an inspired editor and a good friend. We're grateful for the chance to take that idea and make it our own. Once again we'd like to thank Becky Cabaza, our editor at Simon & Schuster, for her support—and her boundless patience. And to our agent, Carol Mann—kudos.

During the creation of this book our fourth child, Benedict, arrived on the scene. We can honestly say that whatever Benedict did to keep us up in the wee hours of the night, he more than made up for as our tiny muse. His older siblings—Magdalen, Helena, and Charles—put up with many boring weekends (and the Blizzard of '96, among other things) while Mom and Dad labored on this book. Thanks, guys.

Finally, we are grateful for the help we received from the Center for Living Democracy, from International Urban Associates, and from the many kind people we met on the Internet.

Contents

Introduction: Making the Ascent

One of the most common complaints made against the media today is that the reporting of bad news—from bloody civil wars across the globe to the seemingly endless series of heinous crimes taking place in our own backyard—seems to dwarf the coverage of good news. But if one is persistent, it is still possible to find stories that stir our hearts to hope, even though such stories may be buried in the back sections of our newspapers or slipped in between the sound bites on the evening news. Take, for instance, the woman who drives a twenty-year-old mobile home into the streets of East Cleveland, braving the frequent sound of gunfire in order to get young people to talk about their anger and their dreams. Or the factory owner whose plant burned to the ground, but who insisted on continuing to pay his workers, including a promised Christmas bonus, while the process of rebuilding began. Or the retired postal worker who, since the mid-1970s, has given away nearly $100,000 to dozens of people, while he and his wife have continued to live in the poorest of neighborhoods.

Who are these people, and what is it that motivates them to undertake such heroic deeds? In the case of the three individuals mentioned above, and of many other local heroes (most of whose actions never make it into the news), the answer is the same: they are guided by moral principles and imperatives that are thousands of years old. If you asked them directly about the sources of their morality, they might become tonguetied—no one wants to sound pompous or smug. But their answers remain the same: the words of ancient sages, prophets, and philosophers have the enduring power to summon us to a higher standard of behavior, to acts of generosity and self-sacrifice and compassion.

As concern about the fraying of our social fabric continues to mount, many of us are wondering what happened to the moral values that seem to be conspicuously absent from our lives. It isn't an easy subject to discuss; when we talk about morality we tend to become awkward and self-conscious. At some point in our history, morality got a bad name, becoming associated with the stuck-up prigs known as the Victorians, or with the picture-perfect 1950s family headed by Ozzie and Harriet. Besides, we have been told for decades that old-fashioned morality was hopelessly out-of-date. In its place arose a philosophy of relativism, which says that morality is what each individual creates for himself. The most extreme formulation of relativism, of course, is the slogan "If it feels good, do it!" But the problem with relativism is that we are becoming sick of the "morality" of terrorists, drug lords, white-collar criminals, racists, and their ilk.

While most people today are willing to concede that previous generations erred on the side of a dry, conventional moralism, there is a widespread feeling that we have moved too far in the opposite direction, that we have lost our bearings and desperately need some form of moral wisdom by which to navigate through the complex waters of our lives. Thus it is no longer taboo to speak of ideas like virtue, character, and goodness. At the same time—thanks to an educational system that scorned the wisdom of the past—there is tremendous ignorance about the sources of moral vision.

A wise man once said: "To get away from old things passing themselves off as tradition it is necessary to go back to the furthest past—which will reveal itself to be the nearest present." In other words, by going back to the sources of the great moral traditions, we can rediscover just how fresh and relevant they are for our own time. That, at any rate, is the premise of this book. We have gone back to the furthest past to cull quotations from the original texts—scriptures, treatises, and practical guides to behavior—and we have searched the nearest present to find stories about people who continue to be inspired by traditional values.

Despite the many significant differences between them, the ancient traditions, from Greek philosophy to the major religions, all agreed that morality was objective, that the idea of good and evil was firmly rooted in human nature itself. Central to each of these traditions was something the Chinese called the *Tao*, which might be translated as the Way, or the Road. In order to stay on the Way, one was required to heed the compass, or set of moral principles, that kept us from losing our bearings in the fog and landing in ditches and quagmires.

Another universal idea was that the moral path required discipline and self-sacrifice. Doing the right thing is seldom the easiest or most natural option. But just as we know that the pain of physical exercise is a necessary means to the end of health and good conditioning, so moral exercises were seen as means to a state of inner peace and contentment. Again and again the ancient traditions promise that if you serve the needs of others you will find that you have received something valuable in return. The Way might lead up steep mountain paths, but the views from the top are exhilarating.

The modern feeling that morality is always about repression or merely negative values was completely alien to the great moral traditions. While it is true that many of the commandments were couched in "Thou shalt nots," it must be remembered that the positive side of these commandments was their call to greater love. It has been remarked that if you substitute the words "Love does not" for "Thou shalt not," the Ten Commandments can be seen in a new light. Love does not kill. Love does not steal. Love does not bear false witness.

Nonetheless, it must be said that if traditional morality is based on the radiance of love and goodness, it can also seem sharp-edged and challenging to our contemporary sensibilities. The moral precepts from Mount Sinai and Galilee and Mecca are not based on notions like "self-esteem" and nurturing "the child within"; nor do they foist responsibility for wrongdoing onto society or the traumas of youth. The commandments are not suggestions for fleeting "random acts of kindness" that can be practiced in one's spare time, but bracing calls to a lifetime commitment. Above all, the ancients knew that the moral life was grounded in the dozens of ordinary daily actions we take—that the little things in the end add up to big things. In the end, when we reach the mountaintop, we will have formed our character, our soul, and we will know that our lives have meant something.

In compiling this volume, we decided that a book divided into sections according to abstract ideas like "honesty" or "courage" would have little bearing on the way we actually lead our lives. Instead, we have arranged the material in sections according to the major phases of human life, from childhood and family life through marriage, work, education, and on to death and posterity. Nearly all of our moral decisions are made in specific, concrete circumstances—in our bedrooms, classrooms, and offices. These are the stages through which we all must pass.

It goes without saying (but we'll say it anyway) that this book makes no pretension to being a comprehensive listing of moral ideas and precepts. We have kept to the large central ideas of each moral tradition, rather than delving into the more specific differences between traditions.

Each section begins with a brief introduction, and then moves into a series of quotations. The quotes include the sayings from the sources of moral thought—the scriptures, philosophical texts, and other founding documents. We have endeavored to select material from all of the world's major religions: Judaism, Christianity, Islam, Buddhism, Hinduism, Confucianism, and several strands of the Native American traditions. There are also many quotations—from traditional sayings to the wisdom of the greatest poets and thinkers—that extend and develop the original tradition over the centuries.

Some readers may be inclined to wonder why so many of the quotations come from religious sources. The answer is simple: through most of human history, morality has emerged from a religious matrix. Even the Greek philosophers developed their moral ideas through a dialogue with the myths of the Olympian gods. For better or worse, the idea that morality can be constructed from scratch, out of the human mind alone, is a very recent notion.

We found the quotations for this book in a variety of sources, from modern translations of ancient texts to specialized studies in comparative religion and philosophy to collections of proverbs and folk sayings. Since this isn't a work of scholarship, we have not burdened the text with detailed citations. However, most of the works cited can easily be found in public libraries. In quoting from the Bible, we have deliberately chosen to use several different translations. While we prefer the King James Version, we realize that many people prefer contemporary language—hence the use of multiple translations.

Finally, each section concludes with a story or two from the present, or the recent past, which illustrates the way the moral traditions continue to inspire people today. All the stories grow out of the life experiences of the many individuals who contributed them. The contributors come from varied backgrounds and many walks of life. Many of these individuals responded to the call for stories we placed on dozens of sites on the Internet. Their generous response to that call amazed and gratified us. We have changed names to protect the privacy of the storytellers.

We hope the result is a rich trove of wisdom, information, and inspiration—all geared to the challenges we face in our daily lives.

We would like to thank all those who responded to our calls for stories. In particular we are grateful to the following for sharing their lives with us: David Bovenizer, David Cullen, M. A. Gorman, A. G. Harmon, Cheri Jacobs, Andrew Kimbrell, Jan Krist, Caroline Langston, Carmen Leal-Pock, Jack Leax, Michael Mata, Keith Miller, John Pierce, and Linda Ross.

TREASURING CHILDREN — AND PARENTS — IN A BUSY WORLD

A child is born. No other moment in life can quite match the range of emotions that attend this event, from the anxiety and pain of birth to the ecstatic joy of welcoming a bright new presence among us. The birth of a child brings renewal and hope; it extends the human race through time. "Be fruitful, multiply, fill the earth," God says to Adam and Eve. But mixed in with the joy of new life is the awareness of what an awesome responsibility has been laid upon the parents: the need to care for the child's every need, physical, mental, and emotional. The sacrifices and the hard work demanded of a parent can often seem unbearable. Whatever role genetics may play, we know how immensely important the family environment is to the healthy development of a child. We are the living examples that our children will imitate.

The family has been called the school of charity, because it is our first and most important moral training ground. We choose all other relationships; we don't choose our families. And though people do walk away from their families, we have a deep instinct that tells us we must struggle to live together in peace and love. The fact that most families do not live up to the ideal does not absolve us as parents, and children, of the imperative to love and to forgive.

In our society, children are in greater jeopardy than they have been for a hundred years. But, contrary to frequent news reports, not all the threats come from the pervasiveness of violence and sexual promiscuity in our society. The generation that tried to satisfy itself with the idea that parents could get away with spending "quality time" with their children is now having second thoughts. These parents are realizing that their children are slipping away from them. The ancient moral traditions all went to great pains to set out the obligations between children and parents. The wisdom contained in these sayings is perennial, as fresh today as when first uttered.

✳

God blessed [Adam and Eve], saying to them, "Be fruitful, multiply, fill the earth and conquer it."

Genesis 1:28

✳

Honor thy father and thy mother.

Exodus 20:12

Train a child in the way he should take, and when he is old, he will not depart from it.

Proverbs 22:6

At this time the disciples came to Jesus and said, "Who is the greatest in the kingdom of heaven?" So he called a little child to him and set the child in front of them. Then he said, "I tell you solemnly, unless you change and become like little children you will never enter the kingdom of heaven. And so, the one who makes himself as little as this little child is the greatest in the kingdom of heaven. Anyone who welcomes a little child like this in my name welcomes me."

Matthew 18:1–5

The great man is he who does not lose his child's-heart.

Mencius

There are three degrees of filial piety. The highest is being a credit to our parents; the second is not disgracing them; the lowest is being able simply to support them.

Confucius

Never promise something to a child and not give it to him, because in that way he learns to lie.

The Talmud

What the child says in the street is his father's words or his mother's.

The Talmud

The branch sprung from violence has no tender twig.

Ecclesiasticus 40:15

Thy Lord hath decreed that ye worship none save Him, and (that ye show) kindness to parents. . . . Lower unto them the wing of submission through mercy, and say, "My Lord, have mercy on them both as they took care of me when I was little."

The Koran

Give me a child for the first seven years, and you may do what you like with him afterwards.

St. Francis Xavier

It is easier for a father to have children than for children to have a real father.

Pope John XXIII

I think it must be somewhere written, that the virtues of the mothers shall be visited on their children as well as the sins of the fathers.

Charles Dickens

The Child is father of the Man.

William Wordsworth

What was wonderful about childhood is that anything in it was a wonder. It was not merely a world full of miracles; it was a miraculous world.

G. K. Chesterton

To understand a parent's love: have a child.

Chinese proverb

When men abandon the upbringing of their children to their wives, a loss is suffered by everyone, but perhaps most of all by themselves. For what they lose is the possibility of growth in themselves for being human which the stimulation of bringing up one's children gives.

Ashley Montagu

The hand that rocks the cradle is the hand that rules the world.

William Ross Wallace

A parent should never make distinctions between his children.

The Talmud

Whoever teaches his son teaches not only his son but also his son's son—and so on to the end of generations.

The Talmud

When a father complains that his son has taken to evil ways, what should he do? Love him more than ever.

Israel ben Eliezer (Ba'al Shem Tov)

The more important thing a father can do for his children is to love their mother.

Theodore Hesburgh

The Heart of the Ten Commandments is to be found in the words: *Revere thy father and thy mother.* The problem I as a father face, is why my child should revere me. Unless my child will sense in my personal existence acts and attitudes that evoke reverence—the ability to delay satisfactions, to overcome prejudices, to sense the holy, to strive for the noble—why should he/she revere me?

Abraham Joshua Heschel

For millions of men and women the family is the one and only setting in which human relationships are not governed predominantly by considerations of bargaining.

E. L. Mascall

Wisdom leads us back to childhood.

Blaise Pascal

My mum was a single parent, and in the small English village in which we lived during the sixties that was no small feat. With high hopes for the future, she had emigrated to Canada, met and married my father and had my brother and me in quick succession. Then my father up and left, leaving her with two small children (I was still an infant and my brother a toddler), no income, no job, no family nearby, and few friends.

One day, returning from the store where she had spent the last of her money on food and diapers, she discovered her furniture lying higgeldy-piggedly out on the street outside her apartment building. Pinned to the door was a notice informing her that she had been evicted because she was behind on her rent. Standing there in the street with my brother by the hand and me in her arms, she was faced with an excruciating decision. Either stay and face possible homelessness and poverty, or move back to her parents' home and suffer the stigma of being an abandoned wife. With characteristic courage, she chose the latter because, she told me years later, "a child needs the love of a family."

We lived with my grandparents until I was eight years old. During that time, my mother worked night and day and saved every penny she could so we could buy a house. She even decided to quit smoking so she could put by the money she spent on cigarettes towards a down payment. Those first eight years were very difficult ones for my mother. Not only did she feel like a failure after the dramatic collapse of her bid for independence and a new life in Canada, but she was regarded with disapproval by many people in the village. There were rumors that she had never been married and that my brother and I were illegitimate. One couple even volunteered to adopt my brother and me because, presumably, they felt that my mum was an unfit mother. When I asked her, years later, how she could possibly have found the strength to carry on, she looked surprised and said, "Because I had you and John to care for. Why else?" Now I am a mother myself, I can understand her remarkable courage. I, too, would do anything for my children. But in those years after we had moved into our own home and she was working all the time, I felt only hurt and resentment at her long absences. During my adolescent years, I frequently clashed with my mother, accusing her, amongst other things, of not loving me. Now I have children of my own, I have finally learned to understand and appreciate my mother. She gave up everything in order to provide for us—marital love, independence, leisure, financial security.

Recently, she came to visit me in the States. Watching her hold my newborn son against her shoulder and seeing the tender way in which she cupped his soft little head in her palm, I realized that she must have held me in the same way. I was overcome with emotion. All the love a mother lavishes on her child, I thought. All the sacrifices she makes. And we, as children, take it for granted. It was then that I realized that that is what love is all about. To give and not to count the cost. My father may have abandoned me and my brother, but my mother had hung in there. It brought to mind the ancient Jewish proverb which says, "God could not be everywhere, so he made mothers."

✳

One of my earliest memories is of sitting in the back of a little nine-foot aluminum rowboat, watching my father row me out into Lake Erie. I was barely three years old at the time, and I can still remember the feel of the bulky orange life jacket that engulfed my small body. We lived in an apartment complex near the water, and my father rowed for exercise and pleasure. One day my father took me out in the rowboat despite the vigorous protests of my mother, who warned him of dangerous conditions as she pointed out the dark storm clouds moving in from the north. But my father, who had a boyish, reckless streak in him, was not to be denied.

When the wind began to toss the boat, and the rain came down, and the waves threatened to swamp the boat, I said to my father: "What should I do, Daddy?"

"Just hold on tight, Peter," he said. "We'll be okay."

According to my father, I was completely satisfied with this answer. I held on for dear life continuing to look at him with trusting eyes. Still, the waves kept on sloshing over the side until the water had crept up to my knees. All I remember is that the water felt incredibly cold, but not cold enough to make me lose faith in my father. Just before the rowboat capsized, my father managed to get it ashore. He scooped me out, pulled the boat onto the beach, and phoned my mother from a nearby house to have her pick us up. When she arrived, she was clearly worried, and upset that her prophecy had been fulfilled. My father only gave a sheepish smile. As my mother clasped me to her with a grip as all-encompassing as the life jacket, I thought it all a wonderful adventure and wondered what the fuss was all about. With my dad there, it had never even entered my head that we were in any serious danger.

Another powerful memory that I cherish is of something that took place a few years later, when we had moved to Long Island. In the intervening years, I had begun to suffer from acute bouts of asthma, and on the humid north shore of Long Island, I was frequently bedridden with bronchitis and recurrent asthma attacks, literally fighting for breath. My father, too, had had asthma from an early age, and, knowing what a terrifying feeling it is to be slowly suffocating to death, would sit on the side of my bed every night, reading from the Bible. The words he read were words of comfort, words that called us to trust in God's love and his healing power. Despite the power of these words, however, it was not so much the content of what my father read, but rather the loving, quietly confident sound of his voice that brought me true solace. It wasn't until I was older that I knew that my father had spoken from experience, that he, too, had fought for breath as a child, that he had almost died in Mexico City where he had gone as a college student because the air was dry enough to keep him alive. When I heard my father tell me about a compassionate father in heaven, I had little difficulty in trusting that he was telling me the truth.

In recent years many studies have focused on the importance of fathers for the healthy development of children. Without taking anything away from the immeasurable love of a mother, it remains true that a father's attentive presence is crucial to a child's maturation. My wife grew up without a father, and having held her in my arms while she wept at the loss of him and at the terrible insecurity that is the legacy he left her, I now have gained insights into the real-life experiences behind these statistics. The inner confidence that I drew from my father has sustained me through many hard times. Despite my father's faults—faults which I now see from the perspective of being a father myself—he nonetheless mediated the Father's love to me. A love that could demand trust. A love that could face danger—the danger of drowning and serious illness. A love that was all-sustaining. While many of my own generation agonize over whether they can make the sacrifices that children require, I found myself embracing fatherhood.

My eldest son, whom I named Peter, looks up to me from his sickbed, pale and feverish and afraid. But the asthma he has unavoidably inherited from his father and grandfather is not his only legacy: I read to him from the Bible, and other books, and I find my voice falling into a quiet rhythm—a rhythm that is not entirely my own.

MARRIAGE FOR
BETTER FOR WORSE

As with the birth of a child, marriage often begins in the heady joy of romantic love and then runs smack into the more mundane give-and-take of daily life. In an age dominated by the desire for instant gratification, phrases like "for better for worse" and "till death do us part" have somewhat doubtful meanings. There has even been serious discussion recently about people having "starter" marriages, the way they might buy a "starter" house and then trade upward. We may have moved beyond the blandness of Ward and June Cleaver, and brought about a healthier sense of equality in marriage, but most people suspect that we have chucked the baby out with the bathwater. It's difficult to avoid cynicism when it comes to an institution as battered as marriage.

But to the ancients, marriage was not something to be treated casually. The ideal, of course, is to be found in the biblical image of two individuals becoming "one flesh"—not only in the sexual sense, but in terms of the knitting together of personalities. It is a process that requires large measures of forbearance, patience, and common sense. In short, what is required is a total commitment, then a lifetime of fidelity to that commitment. Anything less, the ancients thought, implied a love that had conditions attached to it—a contradiction in terms.

Another belief common to the moral traditions is that marriage should not merely be a closed unit, an inward-looking relationship, but should turn to face the world, starting with the bearing and raising of children, and then moving outward to the larger community.

There are also innumerable proverbs and sayings about marriage that are marked by an earthy sense of humor, a vivid awareness of the foibles and follies that attend the married state. Marriage and laughter go together—or ought to.

Yahweh God said, "It is not good that the man should be alone. I will make him a helpmate."

Genesis 2:18

Therefore shall a man leave his father and his mother, and shall cleave unto his wife: and they shall be one flesh.

Genesis 2:24

Be subject to one another out of reverence for Christ. Wives, be subject to your husbands, as to the Lord. . . . Husbands, love your wives, as Christ loved the church and gave up himself up for her. . . . Even so husbands should love their wives as their own bodies. . . . "For this cause shall a man leave his father and mother, and shall be joined unto his wife, and they two shall be one flesh." This is a great mystery.

Ephesians 5:21–31

God creates new worlds constantly—by causing marriages to take place.

Zohar

Love your wife as you love yourself—and honor her more.

The Talmud

I N. take thee N. to be my wedded Wife [Husband], to have and to hold from this day forward, for better for worse, for richer for poorer, in sickness and in health, to love and to cherish, till death us do part, according to God's holy ordinance; and thereto I plight [give] thee my troth.

The Book of Common Prayer

Love does not consist in gazing at each other but in looking together in the same direction.

Antoine de Saint-Exupéry

God has set the type of marriage everywhere throughout creation. Every creature seeks its perfection in another. The very heavens and earth picture it to us.

Martin Luther

The kindest and the happiest pair will find occasion to forbear; and something, every day they live, to pity and perhaps forgive.

William Cowper

The marriage state, with and without the affection suitable to it, is the completest image of Heaven and Hell we are capable of receiving in this life.

Sir Richard Steele

The state of marriage is one that requires more virtue and constancy than any other; it is a perpetual exercise of mortification.

St. Francis de Sales

To live with someone and to live in someone are two fundamentally different matters. There are people in whom one can live without living with them, and vice versa. To combine both requires the purest degree of love and friendship.

Johann Wolfgang von Goethe

The goal of our life should not be to find joy in marriage, but to bring more love and truth into the world. We marry to assist each other in this task. The most selfish and hateful life of all is that of two beings who unite in order to enjoy life. The highest calling is that of the man who has dedicated his life to serving God and doing good, and who unites with a woman in order to further that purpose.

Leo Tolstoy

It is not marriage that fails; it is the people that fail. All that marriage does is to show people up.

Harry Emerson Fosdick

A successful marriage demands a divorce: a divorce from your own self-love.

Paul Frost

Marriage is an act of will that signifies and involves a mutual gift, which unites the spouses and binds them to their eventual souls, with whom they make up a sole family—a domestic church.

Pope John Paul II

My husband and I met at college—I was nineteen, he was twenty-one. Looking back from the vantage point of my thirties, I now see how frighteningly young we were. We got married two weeks after I graduated. I remember my mother's worried expression when I told her David and I were engaged. She didn't say it, but I knew she was thinking how inexperienced I was, how blissfully ignorant of all the pitfalls that might lie ahead, how I had no idea that the statistics on college marriages were against us. I remember dismissing her fears, putting them down to a mother's overprotective love and the cynicism of middle age. I couldn't foresee any force either in heaven or on earth that could come between David and me. And although I was experienced enough to know that other couples had their difficulties, I was convinced that we would not be among them. Wasn't love supposed to conquer all? Twelve years and four children later I can look back on my naïveté and smile. My mother was right to worry.

The first difficulty to hit me head-on was the transition from college to the more mundane life of a housewife. After spending four years doing basically what I wanted (including extensive travel in Europe) as long as I made my grades, I suddenly found myself shackled to a small apartment in a strange town, with no friends, no car, and an infant who never seemed to sleep. Suddenly I had no freedom at all. The dream of living as David's wife seemed to have suddenly transformed itself into a living nightmare. I was lonely—David seldom made it home from work much before seven—and chronically sleep-deprived. On top of that, I had always hated housework, regarding it as infinitely inferior to other, more intellectual work.

But the worst thing of all was that I felt that I had suddenly lost my identity. In college I was regarded by both my professors and my friends as one of the more promising students, one who would doubtless go on to do great things. Now here I was changing diapers, washing dishes, and sweeping floors instead of working at the high-powered publishing job that I had dreamt of in college. When I look back, I can honestly say that if it hadn't been for David's abiding faith in me our marriage would never have survived. Faced with a wife who had suddenly changed from a high-spirited, bright, and witty young woman into someone who would spend hours sitting in a chair crying, he responded with love and understanding. There was many a night when he would walk our daughter, sometimes until dawn, despite his grueling work schedule. But it wasn't only his willingness to help out in whatever way he could that sustained me, it was his repeated assurances that looking after a home and baby did not, and should not, define my being. He encouraged me to learn how to drive so that I wouldn't be so house-bound, so that I could get out from time to time on my own. He suggested that I learn how to touch-type so that I could write articles for journals (I was a literature major and had been writing short stories since the age of four).

Gradually, little by little, my confidence returned. I began to recognize myself again. One night, when our daughter was two years old and I had gotten a job teaching at a small liberal arts college, I confronted David. "Why?" I asked. "Why did you hang in there?" "Because I love you, Julia," he said simply. His response still echoes in my mind and heart ten years later, and tells me more about the nature of marriage than any statistic, sermon, or self-help book could ever do. My husband had faith in his love for me, faith that the girl he married could sustain the travails of marriage, faith that she could sustain the growing pains of the surrender of romantic love for a more mature love—a love that expanded to encompass my children and my students. *Do I have faith in me?*

After a hiatus of six years, during which I taught and published several books, we have just had our fourth child. He is called Daniel and is very beautiful. Once again, David and I find ourselves walking a colicky baby around a darkened house; once again we find ourselves changing soggy diapers. But that's as far as the similarity to our experience as first-time parents goes. Somehow, over the twelve years of our marriage, we have become a team, partners who love and respect each other. It doesn't mean that life can't be hard sometimes, but I know that together we can face whatever difficulties may lie ahead. After all, we both swore to love and honor each other "for better for worse."

Julia is right: we were very young when we first met and not much older when we got married. It's true that we were naïve and overconfident: the young and the romantically involved usually are. But we were also determined. You see, both of us grew up in homes that had been broken apart by divorce. We resolved that we were not going to repeat the mistakes of our parents.

Only months into our married life we learned that we were not immune from the conflicts and forces that had plagued our parents. (Our love and sympathy for them increased accordingly.) Julia was alone in the apartment with our firstborn, experiencing huge mood swings—not only the joy of motherhood but also the depression that comes with physical exhaustion, loneliness, and boredom. I was coming home late from work, dog tired and guilty about what Julia had to face every day.

It seemed that we were caught in the proverbial Catch-22 scenario: we were doing the right thing, but it was placing an enormous strain on our marriage. On the one hand, we had rejected the cultural trend that was telling us to put off having children until we were well established in our careers; there was, we believed, a strong temptation to selfishness in the "double income, no kids" lifestyle. On the other hand, it was hardly sufficient to ask Julia to be patient while her creative energies were stuck in limbo.

In our worst moments, it seemed that the biblical statement about a man and a woman becoming "one flesh" in marriage was nothing more than a bad joke. All too often Julia and I remained stubbornly separate. But there was another biblical passage that flitted through my mind from time to time. It was from St. Paul's Epistle to the Ephesians, which contains the well-known admonition for wives to be "submissive" to their husbands. That command has earned St. Paul a reputation for being a male chauvinist, but I discovered that it is only part of what he says about marriage. He goes on to tell husbands that they must love their wives as Christ loves his church, and that they must sacrifice themselves for their wives. The longer I thought about this, the more I realized that becoming "one flesh" required us to bear each other's burdens. In my heart I knew that Julia's sacrifices were far greater than mine. So, rather than leaving Julia to take care of the baby and the home, I had to do my share of those labors (something that rarely happened in our parents' generation). And I had to make it possible for her to use her mind and talents as I was doing in my work.

That's why I knew I had to walk the baby in the night and become an expert in feeding, changing, and bathing techniques. Of course, it didn't take long for me to realize how much joy I could experience by spending these moments with my child. Sharing these joys and labors didn't solve all our problems, but it established a pattern that has strengthened our marriage and our love.

Glossy magazines and TV ads constantly tell us that we can have it all—kids, marriage, career—by carefully planning our lives: postponing children, scheduling romantic getaways, starting IRA accounts. But the truth is that life is far more messy, and potentially more rewarding, than these messages can comprehend. We can only "have it all" if we are prepared for late nights, leaky diapers, and a million daily sacrifices. Chauvinist pig or not, I'm convinced St. Paul knew something that *Cosmo* doesn't.

3

MAKING FRIENDS IN A WORLD FULL OF STRANGERS

Having a friend is like having an anchor, a point of reference amid the shifting allegiances and acquaintances of life. A friend is someone with whom we can be completely natural; the masks we wear for public view can be set aside. Often we choose our friends, but just as often they choose us. Though friendship does not possess the erotic intensity of romantic love, it is a unique and valuable form of intimacy. To our best friends we bare our souls, exposing the most vulnerable and fragile parts of our personality. We do this because we trust our friends; we count on their unconditional love. On the other hand, friends can be our toughest critics and most precious counselors.

Without loyalty, friendship breaks down. When our six-year-old son confided to his friend that his pants had split in the middle of the school day, and this friend then blurted the secret to the rest of the class, our son felt betrayed. And rightly so. When we get in trouble, we expect our friends to come and bail us out. They know that we will do the same for them. Friends implicitly sign mutual-defense treaties.

The truest friendships are based on genuine delight in the other, not on personal vanity or a cliquish mentality. When one is part of a circle of friends, it becomes clear that each member of the circle brings out something special in the others. Friendship does not require people who are identical: often complementary personalities make for the most engaging relationships. But friendship does depend, in the words of the eighth-century theologian Alcuin, on "equality of minds."

✳

If on the journey of life a man cannot find a wise and intelligent friend who is good and self-controlled, let him then travel alone, like a king who has left his country, or like a great elephant alone in the forest.

The Dhammapada

✳

Friendship with a man is friendship with his virtue, and does not admit of assumptions of superiority.

Mencius

When you meet with a man of worth, seek to attain his level; when you meet with a man of worthless character, examine your own heart.

Analects

Two are better than one; because they have a good reward for their labour. For if they fall, the one will lift up his fellow: but woe to him that is alone when he falleth; for he hath not another to help him up.

Ecclesiastes 4:9–10

But Ruth replied [to Naomi], "Do not urge me to leave you, to turn back and not follow you. For wherever you go, I will go; wherever you lodge, I will lodge; your people shall be my people, and your God my God. Where you die, I will die and there I will be buried. Thus and more may the Lord do to me if anything but death parts you from me now."

Ruth 1:16–17

Jonathan's soul became bound up with the soul of David. . . . Jonathan and David made a pact, because [Jonathan] loved him as himself. Jonathan took off the cloak and tunic he was wearing and gave them to David.

1 Samuel 18:1, 3–4

Greater love hath no man than this, that a man lay down his life for his friends.

John 15:13

※

A companion who tells you your faults is better than a companion who hands you a gold coin.

Ibn Gabirol

※

Friendship: one heart in two bodies.

Ibn Zabara, Book of Delight

※

To pull a friend out of the mire, don't hesitate to get dirty.

Israel ben Eliezer (Ba'al Shem Tov)

※

Real friendship is shown in times of trouble; prosperity is full of friends.

Euripides

※

True friendship ought never to conceal what it thinks.

St. Jerome

The best mirror is an old friend.

Traditional saying

I can't be your friend and your flatterer too.

Traditional saying

Friendship improves happiness, and abates misery, by doubling our joy, and dividing our grief.

Joseph Addison

By friendship you mean the greatest love, the greatest usefulness, the most open communication, the noblest sufferings, the severest truth, the heartiest counsel, and the greatest union of minds of which brave men and women are capable.

Jeremy Taylor

A man should keep his friendships in constant repair.

Samuel Johnson

We love ourselves notwithstanding our faults, and we ought to love our friends in like manner.

Cyrus

Great Spirit, help me never to judge another until I have walked two weeks in his moccasins.

Sioux Indian saying

The friendship that can cease has never been real.

St. Jerome

Tell me what company thou keepest, and I'll tell thee what thou art.

Miguel de Cervantes

All kinds of things rejoiced my soul in their [my friends'] company— to talk and laugh and do each other kindnesses; read pleasant books together; pass from lightest jesting to talk of the deepest things and back again; differ without rancor, as a man might differ with himself, and when most rarely dissension arose find our normal agreement all the sweeter for it; teach each other or learn from each other; be impatient for the return of the absent, and welcome them with joy on their homecoming; these and such like things, proceeding from our hearts as we gave affection and received it back, and shown by face, by voice, by the eyes, and a thousand other pleasing ways, kindled a flame which fused our very souls and of many made us one. This is what men value in friends.

St. Augustine

Graduating from a private school with all my friends was something I looked forward to. But this dream was shattered the day my mother announced I would have to go to the local public junior high school for eighth grade. This decision, of course, was financial in nature. My father had lost his job and my parents could no longer afford private school.

I spent the summer contemplating just how awful my school year was going to be. Though not shy, I was still worried about the fact that I had to make new friends. I soon found that I should not have wasted my time worrying. I discovered many students with common interests. On the first day I found a friend, Mary, who helped to ease my transition into public school. Mary and I both sang in the choir. She was very popular and helped to open doors that might have remained firmly shut to me in an adolescent world dominated by cliques.

One day my friend announced she was having a slumber party for her birthday. Since I had never attended a slumber party, I was thrilled. Finally the momentous Friday evening arrived. As our car pulled up to the house, I scrambled out and ran up the walkway clutching my sleeping bag to my chest. I rang the bell and waited impatiently for Mary to answer.

I can still see the face of Mary's mother as she opened the door. Every hair was in place; she looked like a June Cleaver clone. She gave me a quizzical glance and proceeded to let me know that my friend could not come out this evening. She was having a slumber party.

I broke in to tell her I had been invited. She repeated that I could come over tomorrow but not tonight. I began to panic: Had she heard me correctly? Had I imagined the friendship and the invitation? I became queasy, and tears welled up in my eyes.

I then heard Mary asking who was at the door. Before her mother could answer, Mary rounded the corner and stood in the doorway. She had only to look at me to see there was a problem. "Mom, what's happening?" she said. After a brief hesitation her mom replied, "Yolanda is here to visit and I told her to come back tomorrow because you are having a party."

A flush of embarrassment flooded Mary's face. "I invited Yolanda to my party, Mom. She's my friend and I want her here." "This is a sleepover," replied her mother. "I can't have a colored girl sleeping in our house."

I could not believe what I was hearing. It was as if someone had punched me in the stomach. How could this be? What had I done? Why did the color of my skin matter?

I thought about calling my mom to come and get me. But the battle raged on between Mary and her mother. Finally Mary declared: "Yolanda is my friend. If she can't stay, no one stays. I won't have my party without her."

I was stunned. Mary was willing to have over a dozen girls call home and say the party had been canceled. A look of consternation passed over her mother's face, and I saw it harden into a set mask. "All right. If that's what you want, go tell the girls."

One by one the girls assembled with their belongings, waiting for their rides home. I was suddenly nervous that I would be blamed for the disastrous end of the planned festivities. By Monday the aborted birthday party was the hot topic of conversation at school, and most of the girls—with the exception of Mary—did not remain friends with me.

The hurt took a long time to heal. Whenever I saw Mary's mother I was filled with a confused mixture of emotions. Over the next few years I spent many hours with Mary at school; our friendship was so strong that Mary's mother could do nothing to prevent it. One day Mary invited me back to her home. Despite my fears of another expulsion, Mary's mother did not object, and I became a frequent visitor. Little by little the barriers between her mother and me began to melt, and she was able to see me not as "the little colored girl," but as a friend.

Mary and I remained close, even after we had graduated from high school.

I learned about real friendship that year, and it was a lesson I have never forgotten. Mary's behavior exhibited maturity and compassion that were far beyond her years. I have been blessed with many friends over the years. What I learned that night has helped me to be a faithful friend, and for that I am thankful.

TEACHING AND LEARNING: BRIDGING THE GENERATIONS

As a society, we are constantly making grand claims about the importance of education, about the need for young people to be able to survive in a competitive world, about the importance of mastering the complexities of the Information Age. We praise schoolteachers as unsung—and underpaid—heroes. Yet despite all this stirring rhetoric, how often do we forget that the essence of education is simply the careful preservation of a child's innate wonder? Albert Einstein once said that we should never lose a sense of "holy curiosity." But curiosity, imagination, and wonder are all too easily lost in the welter of information and entertainment that assaults us from the media. And teachers are still underpaid.

Education spans the gap between the past and future; it passes down the knowledge and the skills needed to preserve and strengthen civilization. "Every fresh generation," said Alexis de Tocqueville, "is a new people." The key to a good education, of course, is the teacher herself. Here, too, the most important factor in the teacher's success is not the amount of knowledge he possesses, but the love of learning he embodies. That love is thoroughly contagious.

The teachers who can alter the course of a life are rare and extremely precious. They are selfless people, full of empathy and willing to become involved in the lives of their students. They have to struggle against tremendous odds today. But what they do has a profound impact on what our world will be like in future generations. As Henry Adams said: "A teacher affects eternity; he can never tell where his influence stops."

✳

The fear of the Lord is the beginning of wisdom.

Psalms 111:10

✳

Take fast hold of instruction; let her not go; keep her; for she is thy life.

Proverbs 4:13

✳

When you know a thing, to hold that you know it; and when you do not know a thing, to allow that you do not know it—this is knowledge.

Confucius

Don't limit a child to your own learning, for he was born in another time.

Rabbinic saying

The very world rests on the breath of children in the schoolhouse.

The Talmud

In seeking knowledge, the first step is silence, the second listening, the third remembering, the fourth practicing, and the fifth—teaching others.

Ibn Gabirol

The raft of knowledge ferries the worst sinner to safety.

The Bhagavad Gita

A free curiosity is more effective in learning than a rigid discipline.

St. Augustine

To teach is also to learn.

Japanese proverb

A teacher who can arouse a feeling for a single good action, for one single good poem, accomplishes more than he who fills our memory with row upon row of natural objects, classified with the name and form.

Johann Wolfgang von Goethe

What sculpture is to a block of marble, education is to the human soul.

Joseph Addison

You cannot teach a man anything; you can only help him to find it within himself.

Galileo Galilei

The ink of the scholar is more sacred than the blood of a martyr.

Muhammad

The supreme end of education is expert discernment in all things—the owner to tell the good from the bad, the genuine from the counterfeit, and to prefer the good and the genuine to the bad and the counterfeit.

Samuel Johnson

The true teacher defends his pupils against his own personal influence.

Bronson Alcott

Everything depends on the person who stands in the front of the classroom. The teacher is not an automatic fountain from which intellectual beverages may be obtained. He is either a witness or a stranger. To guide a pupil into the promised land, he must have been there himself. When asking himself: Do I stand for what I teach? Do I believe what I say? he must be able to answer in the affirmative. What we need more than anything else is not *textbooks* but *textpeople*. It is the personality of the teacher which is the text that the pupils read; the text that they will never forget.

Abraham Joshua Heschel

By the time I was fourteen, I already knew that I wanted to be an historian and that the only place I wanted to study was Oxford University. At fifteen I visited Trinity College, interviewed with a history don there, and decided that that was where I wanted to go. Every building and stone in Oxford breathed antiquity. Even the student lodging I was shown had a slanted floor because it had been built in the fifteenth century and had warped over time.

I returned to my hometown and the mundane routine of high school. But my studies had purpose now. They were my ticket out of the dull industrial town in which I lived, out of my prosaic middle-class upbringing and into the world of Oxford's "dreaming spires," where people were unself-conscious about talking about ideas. Some day, I vowed, I would graduate from Oxford.

One day, several weeks after my visit, I bumped into an English teacher at my school. I didn't know much about him except that he was said to have a temper and had been known to pelt recalcitrant students with chalk and irony. His aim in both was reputed to be deadly. "Ah, Chris," he said. "We're having a little meeting about poetry tonight after school. My office." I remember mumbling some excuse. "No matter," the teacher said. "Just thought you might be interested." For an instant our eyes met, then he strode on. I stood looking after him, puzzled. What had his look meant? It hadn't been critical exactly, just shrewdly appraising, as if he were looking into my soul and weighing it. I was left with the sneaking suspicion that if I didn't take him up on his offer I might regret it for the rest of my life.

The thought nagged me for the rest of the day, so by the time the bell rang to signal the end of classes, I had made up my mind. I would just look in at the meeting. If I didn't like it, I would leave. It was as simple as that . . . or so I thought. Little did I know at the time that that poetry meeting was the beginning of a lifetime love affair with literature, one that would inspire me to write my own books. I did go on to graduate from Oxford, but with an M.A. in English literature, not in history.

"How did you know?" I asked the teacher, now my friend, only a short while ago. In reply, he quoted Galileo: "'You cannot teach a man anything; you can only help him find it within himself.'" Then he smiled. "I just helped you find your true vocation. After all," he said, "that's *my* vocation."

As a beginning graduate student, I was intimidated by the teaching responsibilities that were thrust upon me. The classes were huge, the students uninterested and underprepared for college-level work. I did not know how to handle teaching a lecture hall full of faces whose eyes—on good days—were generally glazed over, if not closed entirely.

I soon discovered the enormity of the task ahead of me. In the second week of classes I gave an impromptu exam consisting only of a map of the world, and asked the students to label as many countries as they could in twenty minutes. An hour into grading their papers, I found myself battling headache and frustration. Two students were unable to locate the United States, no one could find Sri Lanka, and one student apparently thought that Africa was one *really* big country.

I vowed to whip my students into shape. I piled on reading assignments, developed special writing projects, and even required attendance. I spent hours devising clever and ingenious ways to present material that would capture their attention, and presented more graphic materials in class than a Madison Avenue advertising firm trying to steal the Nike account.

As I handed out final exams, I wondered if I had succeeded in reaching any of my students. Three excruciating hours later I collected the final papers and teacher evaluations and left the lecture hall. The news was not good. The papers were mediocre, the exams disappointing, and the teacher evaluations less than flattering.

I walked around the campus on an icy cold winter night, going over the semester in my mind. All my efforts had been in vain; I had failed as a teacher. I left for the semester break determined to ask to be reassigned to research duties. When classes resumed, however, I found that I was stuck with another class of 250. I dragged myself to a new lecture hall, dreading the next four months.

My only goals were to hand out the syllabus, set down some ground rules, and escape. With one last, very deep breath, I lifted my head to address this new set of faces.

The first pair of eyes I saw belonged to one of my former students. He seemed a little uncomfortable under my stare, but then flashed me a huge grin. I saw another familiar face in the far corner, and another in the back. In all, fourteen students from the first semester had registered for the second. I had to turn around and pretend to look for chalk to hide my tears.

After class, the young man with the grin came up to the podium. I asked him if he knew that I would be teaching the class when he signed up for it. He laughed and said, "You weren't the best professor I've ever had, but you knew your stuff." He started to walk out the door, then stopped, turned, and said, "And I knew that you cared."

MAKING A
DIFFERENCE: THE
VALUE OF WORK

Does any aspect of our lives evoke more mixed feelings than work? Our jobs can be gloriously fulfilling, opportunities to give our talents full expression—or they can be seem like prison sentences. And what of those who desperately want a job but have trouble finding one? "Corporate downsizing" has become an all-too-familiar phrase in these times.

Then there are the troubling signs that our work patterns are changing. For much of the twentieth century the dream was that technology would free us from long hours of labor and usher in a new era of leisure, of the cultivation of the mind and heart. But in recent years the trend has been toward workweeks of fifty or sixty hours. Even our leisure time seems more frenetic than it should be. Material standards of living have improved, but at what cost?

The wisdom of the ancients speaks directly to these paradoxes. When Adam and Eve were banished from the Garden of Eden, Adam was told that he would have to earn his keep by the sweat of his brow. But the Book of Proverbs calls work a form of prayer. All moral traditions agree that labor is an expression of the dignity of man. Martin Luther King, Jr., encapsulated this vision when he declared: "If a man is called to be a street sweeper he should sweep streets even as Michelangelo painted, or Beethoven composed music."

What is required, say the ancients and their modern exponents, is a delicate balance—between competition and cooperation; between hard work and the rest symbolized by the Sabbath; between the drive to better oneself and a constant awareness of the needs of the less fortunate. At times keeping this balance can seem like a high-wire act, but with the guidance of our wisest teachers, we can make it to the other side.

To [Adam] Yahweh said . . . Accursed be the soil because of you. With suffering shall you get your food from it every day of your life. It shall yield you brambles and thistles, and you shall eat wild plants. With sweat on your brow shall you eat your bread.

Genesis 3:17–19

You are not to exploit the hired servant who is poor and destitute, whether he is one of your brothers or a stranger who lives in your towns. You must pay him his wage each day, not allowing the sun to set before you do, for he is poor and anxious for it; otherwise he may appeal to Yahweh against you, and it would be a sin for you.

Deuteronomy 24:14–15

Be not made a beggar by banqueting upon borrowing, when thou hast nothing in thy purse.

Ecclesiasticus 18:33

False scales are an abomination to the Lord; but a just weight is his delight.

Proverbs 11:1

Come unto me, all ye that labor, and are heavy laden, and I will give you rest.

Matthew 11:28

If anyone will not work, neither shall he eat.

1 Thessalonians 3:10

To produce things and to rear them,
To produce, but not to take possession of them,
To act, but not to rely on one's own ability,
To lead them, but not to master them—
This is called profound and secret virtue.

Lao-tzu

Wealth destroys the fool who seeks not the Beyond. Because of greed for wealth the fool destroys himself as if he were his own enemy.

The Dhammapada

A man's drive for profit should be prompted by the desire to give charity.

Nahman of Bratslav

The workman's rights always take precedence over those of his employer.

The Talmud

The kings, enjoying ease from their birth, did not know the painful toil of sowing and reaping, and had not heard of the hard labors of the lower people. They sought for nothing but excessive pleasure, and so not one of them had long life.

Confucius

He who does a work that ought to be done, without seeking the fruit of works, and is not attached to the objects of the senses or to works, is called a perfect devotee.

The Bhagavad Gita

Work ye. God will behold your work, and so will the faithful. Ye shall be brought before Him Who knoweth the hidden and the manifest alike; and He will tell you of all your works.

The Koran

Labore est orare. [To work is to pray.]

Motto of the Benedictine Order

God sells us all things at the price of labor.

Leonardo da Vinci

If a man is called to be a street sweeper he should sweep streets even as Michaelangelo painted, or Beethoven composed music. He should sweep streets so well that all the host of heaven and earth will pause and say, here lived a great street sweeper who did his job well.

Martin Luther King, Jr.

❧

We work not only to produce but to give value to time.

Eugène Delacroix

❧

Love labour: for if thou dost not want it for food, thou mayst for physic. It is wholesome for thy body, and good for thy mind. It prevents the fruits of idleness which many times comes of nothing to do, and leads too many to do what is worse than nothing.

William Penn

❧

To be idle and to be poor have always been reproaches, and therefore every man endeavors with his utmost care to hide his poverty from others, and his idleness from himself.

Samuel Johnson

No nation can prosper till it learns that there is as much dignity in tilling a field as in writing a poem.

Booker T. Washington

✳

Work is the natural exercise and function of man. . . . Work is not primarily a thing one does to live, but the thing one lives to do. It is, or should be, the full expression of the worker's faculties, the thing in which he find spiritual, mental and bodily satisfaction, and the medium in which he offers himself to God.

Dorothy L. Sayers

✳

Not long ago I became the victim of what the corporate world euphemistically calls downsizing. Suddenly, after years of fulfilling (if exhausting) work, I found myself out of a job and thinking of my mortgage payments with dread. While I had enjoyed working with most of my colleagues, I quickly learned a hard lesson about the impersonal nature of large corporations, as I was let go without ceremony. The whole experience left me bitter and prone to self-pity. The anger and resentment I felt poisoned the atmosphere of my home.

A few months after I lost my job, I found myself pouring out my woes to a Jewish friend. After patiently hearing me out, he poured me another drink and began telling me the story of Aaron Feuerstein. Mr. Feuerstein, my friend told me, lived in the economically depressed city of Lawrence, Massachusetts. From his father, Mr. Feuerstein had inherited a twofold legacy: responsibility for an Orthodox synagogue and the family textile mill—Malden Mills. Both had been built by the Feuersteins and had come to define the family. The synagogue represented their strong sense of spiritual identity, the mill their work ethic. In the preceding two years, both temple and mill had burned down. Feuerstein vowed to rebuild. He made sure his employees were paid on time. He even gave them Christmas bonuses and promised them another month's pay. He told his customers that partial production would resume shortly, and got part of his plant back in action within a month.

I asked my friend why Feuerstein would go to such lengths for his employees. According to my friend, Feuerstein said it was a very old saying from the Jewish tradition that kept him strong throughout this ordeal. "When all is moral chaos, this is the time for you to be a mensch." In Yiddish, my friend explained, the word "mensch" means more than just a man. It carries a sense of righteousness. When it comes to religion, being a mensch means being a devoted Orthodox Jew. When it comes to business, it means being totally committed to the good of his employees and the economic health of the part of New England where Malden Mills is located.

I decided to look Feuerstein's story up on the Internet. I found a story that quoted Chuck Henderson, the president of an outdoor equipment company that worked with Malden Mills. According to Henderson, Feuerstein had extended generous credit when Henderson's business was foundering a few years ago. The credit line saved his company, he said. "That's the kind of guy Aaron is," Henderson said. "If he's got half a loaf of bread, he's going to share it around." Feuerstein, the article continued, is even popular with officials of the union that represents 1,300 people at the burned-out plant. Feuerstein is widely known to be a man of his word and is trusted by the union officials and rank-and-file alike. Feuerstein has steadfastly refused to move his textile business south to Mexico, as so many other mills were doing in the area. The desire to rebuild as quickly as possible, he said, is as much about looking after his employees as it is about profits. "They've been with me for a long time," he was quoted as saying. "We've been good to each other, and there's a deep realization of that that is not always expressed, except at times of sorrow."

I found the story of Aaron Feuerstein heartening. Not long after I heard his story, I found another job, for a smaller, more familylike company. My long-suffering family forgave my earlier self-pity with a casual grace that I didn't deserve. While my future security is hardly guaranteed, I sincerely hope that when the next crisis in my life occurs, I, too, will be able to act like a mensch.

At a point in my career when I was having particular difficulty at work, my father reminded me of a story about his grandfather. It has sustained me through many tough times, on a variety of levels.

Jones McWhorter, my great-grandfather, was a husband and father of six. He worked all his life for the railroad company, and through perseverance received the position of section foreman. This job put him in charge of managing a group of men—both white and black—in the maintenance of a thirty-mile stretch of track. By the standards of the day and place—1920s Mississippi—the job was a good one. The salary afforded his family a large Victorian house in town, nice clothes, and a consistent income with which he could plan their future. Jones was widely known for his honesty, diligence, and authority—especially as he exhibited such traits on the job. His position made him a respected man, and the town named the street on which he lived "McWhorter Street."

One day, after about twenty years on the job, McWhorter was approached by his superior. Times were tough, the boss said, and he knew a couple of men who needed work to support their families. Jones, sympathetic, explained that he had no jobs on the line that weren't already filled. The boss nodded, then clarified his position. The two he was speaking about hiring were white men. Jones eased his head back, understanding: his boss meant him to fire two longtime employees, blacks, and hire the two whites. Without bravado, he refused. The black men were two of his best workers, loyal and conscientious, and they needed their jobs in hard times as much as anyone else did. The boss, surprised and angered at such a response from an otherwise cooperative employee, clarified his position even further: if Jones wouldn't fire the two blacks and hire the two whites, Jones himself would be fired, and a man put in his place who would do as he was told. Jones was given time to think.

He knew that if he failed to follow orders his own family might lose everything: house, possessions, and a steady income. In addition, he would lose a job he had labored for years to get, a job he'd put his heart into, a job he loved dearly. The advice he received from friends and relatives—who were annoyed with him for even considering his situation a dilemma—was unanimous: fire the black men, hire the white ones. After all, nothing would be gained by refusing. The two black men were going to lose their jobs; it was just a matter of who would fire them. After much deliberation, which required him to consult the foundations of his deep faith, Jones made up his mind. He went to see his boss.

No amount of time could have prepared the man for Jones's response. He refused to fire the black men, regardless of the consequences. The boss, amazed, told him to reconsider; he would accomplish absolutely nothing by holding such a position. It was foolish, the boss said. Only he—Jones—and Jones's own family would suffer. Jones held his ground.

True to the boss's word, the railroad dismissed Jones McWhorter for insolence. He was replaced by another foreman, whose first act was to fire the two black men and hire the two whites. Jones lost his house in town, the possessions he'd worked to achieve, and his considerable income. He had to move his family from McWhorter Street to a small farm in the country, where he tried to make a living growing crops. He was not a good farmer, and during the fiercest years of the Depression, his family was nearly destitute.

And yet, though he lost the job that had meant everything to him, he brought the same diligence and zeal he'd exhibited as a foreman to his life on the farm. He was said to love the daily tasks, enjoying the demands of his new work without regrets about the old. His farm was no great success, and he was never able to provide his family with anything near the life they'd enjoyed before. But in the final analysis, it was honest work that he enjoyed most, whatever that work's manifestation might be. To Jones McWhorter, work simply had to placed in perspective—within the context of what was right. No job, however much it provided, was worth the cost of basic human decency.

NEIGHBORS: REDISCOVERING COMMUNITY

Like the members of our family, our neighbors are given to us; we don't choose them. This is both a curse and a blessing. The bachelor who can't be bothered to take care of the jungle that once was a lawn; the dysfunctional family that insists on fighting and screaming, inside and outside, day and night; the college students who have turned the house on the corner into Party Central—these are the neighbors who are sent, it seems, to try our souls.

But all the moral and religious traditions insist that knowing and caring for our neighbors is part of a life well lived. As in the family, it is best that we cannot choose our neighbors: by turning strangers into friends, we draw a little closer to the unity we so desperately need in our divided world. If we cannot learn to live with our neighbors, is it any wonder that we suffer from the larger divisions of race, culture, and national identity?

Our restless, mobile society has eroded many of the grand old neighborhoods, in both our cities and our towns. The "For Sale" signs come up and down as we move from place to place. All too often, we smile vaguely as we greet our neighbors in the street, but that is as far as our interest goes. It seems easier to remain anonymous. Sadly, it seems that there are times when only disasters really bring people together.

Neighborliness is made up of small courtesies—the cup of sugar borrowed over the fence, the chance to baby-sit for the harried couple next door, the barbecue that brings young and old together on a warm summer evening. Our neighbors are not always our favorite people, but they belong to us.

Have I done a neighborly act? I am therefore benefited. Let this be always ready to your mind, and never stop. . . . Men have come into the world for the sake of one another. Either instruct them, then, or bear with them.

Marcus Aurelius

Let us be like the lines that lead to the center of a circle, uniting there, and not like parallel lines, which never join.

Hasidic saying

You shall not bear false witness against your neighbor.

Exodus 20:16

Love thy neighbor as thyself.

Leviticus 19:18

Better is a neighbor that is near than a brother far off.

Proverbs 27:10

They helped every one his neighbor; and every one said to his brother, Be of good courage.

Isaiah 41:6

Thou shalt love the Lord thy God with all thy heart, and with all thy soul, and with all thy mind.

This is the first and great commandment.

And the second is like unto it, Thou shalt love thy neighbor as thyself.

On these two commandments hang all the law and the prophets.

Matthew 22:37–40

Just as we love ourselves despite the faults we know we have, so should we love our neighbors despite the faults we see in them.

Israel ben Eliezer (Ba'al Shem Tov)

The love of our neighbor is the only door out of the dungeon of the self.

George MacDonald

From his hilltop farm a Chinese peasant in his rice field saw the ocean swiftly withdrawn, like some prodigious animal crouching for the leap, and knew the leap would be the tidal wave. He saw also that his neighbors working in low fields must be gathered to his hill or swept away. Without a second thought he set fire to his rice-ricks and furiously rang the temple bell. His neighbors thought his farm on fire and rushed to help him. Then, from that safe hill they saw the swirl of waters over fields just forsaken—and knew their salvation and its cost. Afterwards the people of these rice-fields used to go to the temple to worship their neighbor's spirit while he was still alive.

Attributed to Lafcadio Hearn

If a man be gracious and courteous to strangers, it shows he is a citizen of the world, and that his heart is no island cut off from other lands, but a continent that joins them.

Francis Bacon

We make our friends; we make our enemies; but God sends our next door neighbors.

G. K. Chesterton

Regard your neighbor's gain as your own gain, and your neighbor's loss as your loss.

Taoist saying

To love our neighbor in charity is to love God in man.

St. Francis de Sales

You don't live in a world all alone. Your brothers are here too.

Albert Schweitzer

Justice: to be ever ready to admit that another person is something quite different from what we read when he is there, or when we think about him. Or rather, to read in him that he is certainly something different, perhaps something completely different, from what we read in him. Every being cries out to be read differently.

Simone Weil

As an active member of a large and prosperous urban church, I had been talking about the need for parish "renewal" for over a year. Many of us had spoken of the desire we felt to reach out to our city in a more effective, more compassionate way. Finally, we decided that the first step in this process had to come from within, so we formed a small, experimental group to attempt to improve the way we communicated with each other.

The first meeting began with an air of excitement and anticipation. But as we launched into our introductions, it became clear that our words were so careful and superficial that we were still virtually strangers by the time we had gone around the room. I then suggested that we try something different. We should take turns talking for exactly six minutes. During the first five minutes we had to relate those things which popped into our minds out of our past which we thought might have contributed to making us what we are today. In the sixth minute, each person was to relate the happiest experience he or she could recall.

As we started, there was a ripple of nervous laughter. The first person said her happiest experience was her wedding. Next came her husband, and he had no choice but to agree. We were a group primarily made up of couples. After that beginning, most people related positive things about their marriages. By the end of the meeting, I could sense that most of us knew that we were faking our responses. Our first attempt to deepen our sense of community had failed miserably.

Just as we were about to break up, one woman interrupted. "Wait a minute, I haven't said anything." Indeed, this woman had been so quiet I had forgotten she was there. She was a slender woman, about thirty years old. Painfully uneasy, she was nervously clasping her hands. She looked at me hesitantly for a few seconds, then began.

"I've been sitting here feeling awful. I don't have anything in common with you. You talk about happy marriages, and ours has been touch-and-go at best—and often terrible. And only after a lot of good marriage counseling have we come up with a marriage where we are even beginning to find any real communication and love. You speak of happy childhoods. Mine was miserable. My first memory is of my mother's red face screaming at my father to 'get out of our lives.' He left and never came back. I wasn't quite three years old, but I remember feeling afraid and lonely that night. And I've been afraid and lonely every night since.

"As for the happiest moment in my life, I remember one Christmas

Eve when my sister and I were still young girls. We didn't expect anything much for Christmas, not even a tree, because we were very poor after my father left. That night we crept downstairs to start a fire—it was miserably cold in our room. And there, in the corner of the living room, was a Christmas tree with only a few straggly lights on it—the only lights in the room. I remember looking under the tree in the soft glow of those lights and seeing two doll bassinets, each with a soft-skinned dolly in it, and a pink coverlet. We couldn't imagine where my mother had gotten the money for such presents."

The woman had softened as she told her tale. She paused, lost in her memories. Then she looked at us and raised her eyebrows. "And that was the happiest moment in my life. But you know, I realize that I don't belong in this group. I didn't finish high school, and you're all college graduates. I've never known any real acceptance, and you're all successful socially. I guess I just want what you already have."

The rest of us sat there, stunned by the searing intensity of this woman. It was then that I realized that it was *we* who needed what *she* had: the ability to be honest and open, to expose our true feelings and become vulnerable.

A change came over the group at that moment. Several people confessed that they hadn't been totally honest about their lives. The result was that our group grew into a positive force. We discovered a great deal about our "neighbors," and made a first step toward establishing a real community.

7

S E R V I C E :   T H E   G I F T
T H A T   E N R I C H E S
T H E   G I V E R

How many of us, after we have slept, gone to work, eaten our daily meals, and seen to the needs of our families, have time left over to give to others? That, of course, is exactly what performing a service requires: a sacrifice of time and energy from what little we have left. And yet an astonishing number of voluntary and professional organizations in this country and around the world are dedicated to serving the poor, the sick, needy youth, the elderly, prisoners, refugees, the environment, and many other causes. This vast outpouring of aid is one of the most heartening signs at a time when bad news comes thick and fast.

Individuals perform services for others for a variety of motives. However, those who begin their service with the notion that they are superior to the people they are helping quickly find their egos challenged, as several of the stories in this book testify. The people who persevere in service, who learn to see their fellow humans as equals, discover that they receive far more than they give. This unexpected bounty—of receiving more than what is given—can be manifest in countless ways, from the wisdom an elderly person can pass on, to the inner peace and joy of seeing a troubled child's clouded face brighten into a smile.

Once again, those who went before us were unanimous in their belief that service was ultimately a form of thanksgiving for the blessings one has already received. Our lives are linked by webs that have millions of strands, reaching from the past into the present and across the barriers of age, race, religion, and culture. When we serve another's needs, we create a sense of solidarity that renews our hope for a better world.

For I was an hungered, and ye gave me meat: I was thirsty, and ye gave me drink: I was a stranger, and ye took me in: Naked, and ye clothed me: I was sick, and ye visited me: I was in prison, and ye came unto me. . . . In so far as you did this to one of the least of these brothers of mine, you did it to me.

Matthew 25:35–36, 40

A man's true wealth is the good he does in this world.

Muhammad

Teach us, good Lord, to serve Thee as Thou deservest:
To give and not to count the cost;
To fight and not to heed the wounds;
To toil and not to seek for rest;
To labor and not ask for any reward
Save that of knowing that we do Thy will.

St. Ignatius of Loyola

If you stop to be kind, you must often swerve from your path.

Mary Webb

We cannot live only for ourselves. A thousand fibers connect us with our fellow men; and among those fibers, as sympathetic threads, our actions run as causes, and they come back to us as effects.

Herman Melville

The quality of mercy is not strain'd;
It droppeth as the gentle rain from heaven
Upon the place beneath: it is twice bless'd;
It blesseth him that gives and him that takes.

William Shakespeare

It is only through the mystery of self-sacrifice that a man may find himself anew.

Carl Jung

My own self and my pleasures, my righteous past, present and future, may I sacrifice without regard, in order to achieve the welfare of other beings.

Santideva Buddhist saying

No sacrifice is worth the name unless it is a joy. Sacrifice and a long face go ill together.

Mahatma Gandhi

Rings and jewels are not gifts but apologies for gifts. The only true gift is a portion of thyself.

Ralph Waldo Emerson

You give but little when you give of your possessions. It is when you give of yourself that you truly give.

Kahlil Gibran

We do the works, but God works in us the doing of the works.

St. Augustine

✳

If there is any kindness I can show, or any good thing I can do to any fellow being, let me do it now, and not defer or neglect it, as I shall not pass this way again.

William Penn

✳

There never was a person who did anything worth doing that did not receive more than he gave.

Henry Ward Beecher

✳

I don't know what your destiny will be, but one thing I do know: the only ones among you who will be really happy are those who have sought and found how to serve.

Albert Schweitzer

✳

We who lived in concentration camps can remember the men who walked through the huts comforting others, giving away their last piece of bread. They may have been few in number, but they offer sufficient proof that everything can be taken away from a man but one thing: the last of the human freedoms—to choose one's attitude in any given set of circumstances, to choose one's own way.

Viktor Frankl

The service we render for others is really the rent we pay for our room on this earth.

Wilfred Grenfell

The most difficult part is to give. Then why not add a smile?

Jean de la Bruyère

"Sam the Hermit" has lived on the streets of our community for as long as I have lived in it. I met him soon after moving to Los Angeles to pursue work in youth ministry. It was through my efforts with young people that I came to understand the other critical needs of the neighborhood. That's how I decided to go out onto the streets and find ways to help the homeless and the destitute.

Sam was a familiar figure in the neighborhood. I would be hard pressed to say whether Sam is "mentally ill," but it is clear that at one point, he could no longer live within the normal structures of life and preferred to live on his own terms. When he was lucid of mind and approachable, he was very instructive about urban life in general, and my neighborhood in particular. Sam never asked for anything; he never panhandled or pestered anyone. He kept to himself and attended to the welfare of his faithful companion, his dog. You could often see him rummaging for food in the Dumpsters of nearby supermarkets or restaurants. Needless to say, his appearance did not invite contact with him (I think he wanted it that way).

One afternoon, I went to a sandwich shop to have lunch with a colleague. I had eaten more than my fill, so I packed the extra sandwich in a paper bag to eat later. As I returned to my office on foot I came upon Sam. He was sitting against the fence with his dog, seemingly enjoying the sunshine. I thought about the remnant of the sandwich I carried in the bag. Couldn't it be better used to feed the hungry than to indulge my taste buds? I offered my surplus to Sam.

Sam took my bag without comment and opened it to look inside. Then he closed the bag and handed it back to me, saying that he did not want it. I was taken aback by his response: How could he refuse such an act of charity? How dare he reject a kind offer of something he certainly could use? Apparently sensing my thoughts or seeing the offended expression on my face, Sam declared: "Why don't people ever ask what I need?"

That sentence—"Why don't people ever ask what I need?"—rang in my ears. Sensing my interest, Sam went on to explain himself. It was not that Sam was particular about what he ate, he just could no longer eat whatever he wanted or found. Over the years, living on the streets had taken a toll on him; eating food from various sources had damaged his digestive system. Furthermore, should some "kind soul" offer him something that he could not easily digest he would feel obligated to take what was offered to appease the conscience of the benefactor. Then he would either have to find another "poor soul" and share his bounty, or throw it away. Neither option was tenable: he did not have the energy or time to go look for a potential beneficiary, nor did he feel right throwing food away (food that usually was not healthy even for his dog), and carrying the food around did not make sense as it might spoil before he encountered someone who could appreciate it. Everyone, he continued, just assumed what he needed or what was good for him. They looked at him and assumed certain needs that they would take care of. No one, he declared, *ever* asked for *his* input.

Suddenly I realized that the only way you can serve others is to rid your mind of the notion that you are somehow "above" them, offering them charity. After all, I said to myself, I wanted to emulate the example of Jesus, who had been born in a humble manger. The example set by Jesus taught me that compassion does not come from the top down;

it comes from one person standing alongside another, from a consciousness of our common humanity.

Having been humbled (if not humiliated) by Sam the Hermit's words, I meekly asked him: "What do you need, Sam?" This was to become the question that I have asked thousands of times since that afternoon and will continue to ask—not "What can I do for you that will meet *my* need?" but "What do *you* need?"

8

HOLDING THE TRUST:
CITIZENSHIP AND
PUBLIC SERVICE

Anyone who runs for public office today has to be prepared to have his or her life held up to the minutest scrutiny—and to a seemingly endless barrage of innuendoes, half-truths, and outright calumnies. Politics has always been a dirty business, but it is hard to believe that respect for those who hold the public trust has ever been lower. At the same time it may well be true that more public "servants" have been caught serving their own private ends than in any previous era.

The idea of political participation as a dignified and moral act, of government founded on the consent of the governed, goes back to the Greeks. Though the democracy of Athens was rather limited, it did set a standard that would be expanded and enriched over the centuries. Americans are rightly proud of the way their political tradition has extended the scope of individual freedom and civil rights. But today apathy and revulsion threaten the integrity of the political process itself.

Everyone knows that representatives of government can abuse their power through bureaucratic inertia, private greed, or unnecessary intrusions into the privacy and freedom of citizens. According to the moral traditions of the past, those who served the public should be hedged about by a variety of checks and balances. But the one positive ideal that undergirds all of these traditions is the idea of the common good. Perhaps it is time that we once again affirm the value of public service, from the office of dogcatcher all the way up to the presidency.

✳

Judges and officers you shall appoint in all your cities . . . and they shall judge the people with righteous judgment.

Deuteronomy 16:18

✳

You shall not render an unfair decision: do not favor the poor nor show deference to the rich; judge your kinsmen fairly.

Leviticus 19:15

✳

Pray for the welfare of the government, for were it not for the fear of it, people would swallow each other alive.

Ethics of the Fathers

W here there is no vision, the people perish.

Proverbs 29:18

P ut not your trust in princes.

Psalms 146:3

H e who exercises government by means of his virtue may be compared to the north polar star, which keeps its place and all the stars turn towards it.

Confucius

The more laws and order are made prominent,
The more thieves and robbers there will be.

Lao-tzu

W hat . . . does the character of a citizen promise? To hold nothing as profitable to himself; to deliberate about nothing as if he were detached from the community, but to act as the hand or foot would do, if they had reason and understood the constitution of nature, for they would never put themselves in motion nor desire anything otherwise than with reference to the whole.

Epictetus

The precepts of the law are these: to live honorably, to injure no other man, to render to every man his due.

Justinian I

An unstable pilot steers a leaking ship, and the blind is leading the blind straight to the pit. The ruler is like the ruled.

St. Jerome

God changes not what is in a people, until they change what is in themselves.

The Koran

By the accident of fortune a man may rule the world for a time, but by virtue of love he may rule the world forever.

Lao-tzu

For everyone called to the government of nations and empires there are nine cardinal directions to be attended to:

1. Cultivating his personal conduct
2. Honoring worthy men
3. Cherishing affection for, and doing his duty toward, his kindred
4. Showing respect to the high ministers of state
5. Identifying himself with the interests and welfare of the whole body of public officers
6. Showing himself as a father to the common people.

Confucius

The most beautiful thing in the world is freedom of speech.

Diogenes

Who can protest and does not, is an accomplice in the act.

The Talmud

How small, of all that human hearts endure,
That part which kings or laws can cause or cure.

Samuel Johnson

The government in which I believe is that which is based on mere moral sanction . . . the real law lives in the kindness of our hearts. If our hearts are empty, no law or political reform can fill them.

Leo Tolstoy

If, to please the people, we offer what we ourselves disapprove, how can we afterward defend our work? Let us raise a standard to which the wise and honest can repair.

George Washington

Cherish, therefore, the spirit of our people, and keep alive their attention. Do not be too severe upon their errors, but reclaim them by enlightening them. If once they become inattentive to public affairs, you and I, Congress and Assemblies, Judges and Governors, shall all become wolves.

Thomas Jefferson

Man's capacity for justice makes democracy possible. His inclination to injustice makes democracy necessary.

Reinhold Niebuhr

That government is best which governs the least, because its people discipline themselves.

Thomas Jefferson

The most successful government is that which leads its subjects to the highest aim by means of the greatest freedom.

Vincent McNabb

If you want peace, work for justice.

Pope Paul VI

Once I was talking with my father about sacrifices, and whether anyone these days still thought they were important. He told me about a boy he grew up with, and the story impressed me so much that I tell it often, as an example of what human beings can be.

My father's friend was named T. J. Hulsey, and by all accounts he was not an extraordinary boy. He was from a very small Southern town, grew up in the country poverty typical in those regions that never quite recovered from the Depression, and had only the limited education such an environment could afford. He was of average build, average intelligence, quiet disposition, and enjoyed the same activities all the boys of his time and place experienced: hunting, fishing, and simply standing around the town square on hot afternoons. He was not a leader in school or in his group of friends. He was someone everyone knew, but he was not the first person who came to mind.

When the Korean War broke out, T.J., who was around eighteen, was drafted into the service. He spent his time in the army, going through basic training for six weeks, and performing in his usual satisfactory though not stellar manner. When time came for assignments, T.J. was called as one of the men to be sent overseas, to one of the hottest areas of fighting, along the Chinese-Korean border.

Reports of battle could not be overestimated. The Chinese had entered the fray to support the North Korean army; American troops found themselves in the midst of an overwhelming assault from the north. Casualties were a given, deaths an inevitability.

Like all outfits sent into such a situation, T.J.'s group was to hold off the advances as best they could. Unfortunately, the enemy forces were superior in number and position. Through days and weeks of exhausting fighting, T.J. exhibited the skills he had learned in basic training, skills designed to turn men into fighting machines—cold, automatic, efficient. It is said that the best soldiers are those like T.J.—boys whose will can be reconstituted.

A day came when the fighting was particularly fierce. T.J.'s outfit was in steady retreat. The enemy forces were closing in from the front, and threatened to overrun the Americans. Though they fell back from their positions as fast as they could, the Chinese-Korean advance was too fast. T.J.'s platoon was to be overrun in a matter of minutes; their deaths were a certainty. The only way to salvage the situation was for the men to stop trying to defend themselves and make an all-out effort at retreat. Without any fire cover, however, their survival would be nearly impossible.

It was then that this unremarkable boy, who'd never done anything of special note, who'd fought, like all the others, after the fashion of a machine, did something very unlike a machine; something rare; something human.

"Just leave me with your guns," he said, "and all the ammunition you got. I'll hold 'em off while y'all run."

In the little time that was left, there were arguments with T.J.—futile debates to make him change his mind. But in the end, the men knew that unless one of them sacrificed himself, none could live. They agreed, leaving T.J. with their weapons. Under T.J.'s fire cover, the boys made their escape. The noise was tremendous, one of them later reported, and the last time anyone saw T.J., he was standing on a bunker, using an empty rifle as a club to fend off the swarming enemy.

As has happened countless other times in countless other places, when T.J.'s body was returned to the town, people came to meet it. And as for any other boy, there was a dignified service, a flag on the coffin, and heartfelt condolences for the family. But in addition, there were also a large number of military leaders at the funeral, who'd heard of T.J.'s act, and a squadron of pilots who flew over the graveyard in homage. A cascade of letters was delivered, from the families of the boys whose lives T.J. had ransomed. In time, there was also the highest honor a man can receive for military service—a medal commemorating the sacrifice of a life for a country and its people. All this for a quiet fellow of average abilities; someone who, by all accounts, was really an unremarkable boy.

9

MAKING PEACE

The Hebrew word for peace, *shalom*, is a rich, multifaceted term, signifying not merely the lack of conflict, but a deep inner harmony between human beings and between humanity and the world itself. True peace, as the ancients well knew, is a positive value, inextricably related to justice, tolerance, and moral principles. Peace, they knew, could not exist in a vacuum; it requires constant effort and commitment. yes, why LACKiNG peace.

Those who try to bring peace to a divided world have to be strong, courageous people. They also have to have peace within themselves before they can share it with others. The peacemakers stand at the opposite end of the pole from those who say: "I'm not getting involved; it's not my business." As we have learned from many tragic events in our history, the peacemaker is always vulnerable to those who wish to use violence. Peacemaking is a dangerous business.

Our world cries out for peace. Just when many thought that the Cold War had ended, and the major source of fear had been eliminated from our daily lives, a whole host of petty and bitter conflicts seemed to erupt. And not all of these battles are being fought on foreign shores; as the news reports constantly remind us, they continue to exist within our churches, our schools, and our communities. The evils of racism, sexism, and the extreme forms of nationalism and political correctness cut across all boundaries. The person who brings peace to a family turned against itself, the volunteer who rides out amid the gunfire of our urban landscape to get children to put down their weapons, the envoys of peace who shuttle between war-torn nations—all perform the invaluable role of peacemaker. As Jesus says in the Beatitudes: "Blessed are the peacemakers." Or, as a more recent paraphrase has it: "You're blessed when you can show people how to cooperate instead of compete or fight. That's when they discover who you really are."

✳

Peace is important, for God's name is *Shalom* [Peace].

Midrashim: Exodus

A peace which comes from fear and not from the heart is the opposite of peace.

Gersonides

When men war, even God's anger does not frighten them.

Zohar

Great peace have they which love thy law: and nothing shall offend them.

Psalms 119:165

The Lord] shall judge among the nations, and shall rebuke many people: and they shall beat their swords into plowshares, and their spears into pruninghooks: nation shall not lift up sword against nation, neither shall they learn war any more.

Isaiah 2:4

The wolf . . . shall dwell with the lamb, and the leopard shall lie down with the kid; and the calf and the young lion and the fatling together; and a little child shall lead them.

Isaiah 11:6

If a man say, I love God, and hateth his brother, he is a liar; for he that loveth not his brother whom he hath seen, how can he love God whom he hath not seen?

1 John 4:20

Peace hath her victories no less renowned than war.

John Milton

It is forbidden to decry other sects; the true believer gives honor to whatever in them is worthy of honor.

Decree of Asoka

Non-violence is not a garment to be put off and on at will. Its seat is in the heart, and it must be an inseparable part of our very being.

Mahatma Gandhi

We may have all come on different ships, but we're in the same boat now.

Martin Luther King, Jr.

✳

Peace can never be achieved by force. It can only be achieved by understanding.

Albert Einstein

✳

Select your purpose, selfless, without any thought of personal pleasure or personal profit, and then use selfless means to attain your goal. Do not resort to violence even if it seems at first to promise success; it can only contradict your purpose. Use the means of love and respect even if the result seems far off or uncertain. Then throw yourself heart and soul into the campaign, counting no price too high for working for the welfare of those around you, and every reverse, every defeat, will send you deeper into your own deepest resources. Violence can never bring an end to violence; all it can do is provoke more violence.

Mahatma Gandhi

Peace be to the Earth and to the Air!
Peace be to Heaven, peace to the Waters!
By this invocation of peace may peace bring peace.

Atharva Veda

O God, make us children of quietness, and heirs of peace.

St. Clement

Peace is more important than all justice: and peace was not made for the sake of justice, but justice for the sake of peace.

Martin Luther

Without feelings of respect, what is there to distinguish men from beasts?

Confucius

All religions must be tolerated. Every man must get to heaven in his own way.

Frederick the Great

Much violence is based on the illusion that life is a property to be defended and not a gift to be shared.

Henri Nouwen

When brother stands with brother, a war is already half won.

Native American saying

True peace is not merely the absence of tension; it is the presence of justice.

Martin Luther King, Jr.

Lord, make me an instrument of Your peace. Where there is hatred let me sow love; where there is injury, pardon; where there is doubt, faith; where there is despair, hope; where there is darkness, light; and where there is sadness, joy.

O divine Master, grant that I may not so much seek to be consoled as to console; to be understood as to understand; to be loved as to love. For it is in giving that we receive; it is in pardoning that we are pardoned; and it is in dying that we are born to eternal life.

St. Francis of Assisi

Let us not be justices of the peace, but angels of peace.

St. Thérèse of Lisieux

When we let freedom ring, when we let it ring from every village and every hamlet, from every state and every city, we will be able to speed up that day when all God's children—black men and white men, Jews and Gentiles, Protestants and Catholics—will be able to join hands and sing in the words of the old Negro spiritual, "Free at last! Thank God Almighty, we are free at last!"

Martin Luther King, Jr.

I taught junior high school for five years. That period in a child's life can be troubling—for the child and also for everyone who knows the child. There is one particular memory from my own school years whose footfalls I listen to in the corridors of my soul even at this late hour in my life. Like so many other junior high kids, I suffered from a lack of self-confidence, owing not to ugliness or stupidity but to the odd feeling that I was trapped inside the skin of a gawky boy whose hormones and cracking voice crouched by the door to his room and would spring upon him in different and increasingly humiliating ways each morning.

I knew that the tall, dark, and confident boys had no such problems. They were surrounded by adoring associates and seemed to move through the hallways like great ships, pushing to the rocky shore by the force of their personalities those of us who were not blessed with their gifts.

But there is always hope in the heart of a thirteen-year-old boy, even if falsely founded. There were other boys even more gawky, more distressed by hormones and screechy voices, more unsure of their looks, their talents, their places in life, than I. One of those unlucky boys was called Darryl; I took delight in heaping mounds of scorn and hateful laughter upon him. I would follow him down the quiet streets of our town and, aided by one of my own minions, would breathe out "threatenings and slaughter" (as St. Luke wrote of Saul of Tarsus) until Darryl was near to tears. In gym class we exposed him to our locker mates, pulling away his towel so that all could see what we needed to see, that this child—this spectacled, overweight, plain child—was inferior to us. Today, almost thirty years later, my face burns with shame at what we—I—subjected him to.

When, as an adult, I began to take seriously the moral teachings of Christianity, my conscience did not spare me the memory of Darryl running from us in terror. I came to realize that we are all brittle and that my excesses toward him had diminished not only that child, but myself as well. When the high school from which Darryl graduated (I had moved north to another school, a city away, two years prior to graduation) held its twentieth reunion, I was invited to it by another member of that class. It seemed like a God-given opportunity to make amends. I vowed to find Darryl and to ask his forgiveness. But Darryl—this was not really surprising, when I thought about it—was not with his class at that reunion. It seemed that things were going to be just a little more difficult than I had planned. After much searching, I have recently succeeded in tracing Darryl to another state and am close to obtaining his address.

Though my search for forgiveness and reconciliation is not yet complete, I live in the hope that those two gawky boys—Darryl and myself—who have grown into middle age can become the friends that all along they should have been.

A couple of weeks ago, my eight-year-old daughter came home from school with a troubled look on her face. When I asked her what the matter was, she told me that a girl her own age had taunted her about her new coat on the school bus. I was tempted to dismiss the incident, thinking that it was just a mild case of children bickering after a long day at school, until Sarah went on to tell me that Malika had struck her across the face. Malika, it seems, had taken exception to Sarah's attempts to make peace and had lashed out. But it wasn't only her actions that disturbed me, it was her words. "It's a black thing," Malika had told my daughter. "That's what my mom says, and she says you whites are part of the problem." My daughter was not only hurt by Malika's outburst, but was also confused. I asked her if she had ever done or said anything to give offense to Malika. Sarah said no, why should she? I then explained as well as I could that sometimes kids have a rough time at home and in school, and that this sometimes makes them want to take out their anger on others. That what was required was for Sarah to try and understand Malika better, or at the very least not to judge her. My daughter seemed satisfied with this answer, and went to bed somewhat comforted. But as I sat up late that night, I couldn't get the incident out of my head. I knew that it was a small occurrence—the children were, after all, very young and not entirely responsible for their actions—but I couldn't help thinking what might have happened if they had been older. I had seen enough on the evening news to convince me that our schools are filled with kids who think violence is the only way to settle their differences. How can we change that? I found myself wondering. If we can't bring peace to our own homes and classrooms, how can we possibly hope to bring peace to the rest of the world? It seems that the dictum "Charity begins at home" has been thoroughly forgotten in our country. But not, I learned a few days later, by Cheri Jacobs.

I came across her story in a news report on the Internet and was so moved that I decided to call her at the Youth Services Mobile Mediation Project in Cleveland, Ohio. The last four digits of her hotline at the Martin Luther King Civic Center spell out "T-A-L-K." After I had been speaking to her for a few minutes, I understood how apt that was. Cheri Jacobs has committed herself to bringing mediation to the troubled youths in the high schools of East Cleveland. In what she calls her mediation-mobile (a 1977 Itasca motor home she was able to purchase with a grant from the George Gund Foundation), she tours the school district looking for conflict. She encourages youngsters to step inside her mediation-mobile and resolve their differences around a table rather than at one end of a gun or switchblade.

Her mission, Jacobs stresses, is not to tell these young people what to do, but to mediate between them so that they can move toward understanding and peace. "It's all about active listening," she says. "Each side gets heard. I tell them: 'You decide on what the problem is. You identify the solutions.'" Her role model, she explains, is Jesus—"the greatest mediator"—who was not afraid to put himself at risk in order to preach a gospel of love and forgiveness, who did not hesitate to cross into 'enemy'—Samaritan—territory and talk with the troubled woman at the well. Jacobs, who grew up in rural Pennsylvania as the eldest of nine children, developed her faith, and her skills as a mediator, in a close-knit family environment.

Driven by her faith, Cheri Jacobs has no thought for her own safety. The sounds of gunfire, helicopters circling, and police sirens wailing are all too common in her daily experience. But, despite the danger, her concern is unwaveringly centered on the children she comes in contact with every day; children, she says, who more often than not, have a "terrible home life." "I get scared for the kids," she confides. "It's like they're committing suicide out there. They're so cold, so hard, so sad." I ask her if she is ever afraid. No, she says without hesitation. Her Lord will protect her.

After the call, I sat there thinking of the world she had opened up to me. A world of poverty and violence, a world filled with suffering youngsters, desperate for love. I found myself wondering what Cheri Jacobs would do about the conflict between Sarah and Malika. And I knew immediately that she would counsel me to meet with Malika's mother, to reach out to another so that we might find some common ground of understanding. It was then that I remembered her parting words—"You have to *do* love, not just talk it"—and I realized that as long as there are people like Cheri Jacobs in this world, there will be a future for our children, a future for Sarah and Malika.

·

10

NATURE AND THE ENVIRONMENT: LOVING YOUR MOTHER

The Great Law of the Iroquois Nation—one of the founding documents of this fierce and proud Native American people—states that every decision made by the tribal council must be considered in terms of its impact on the next seven generations. Thinking ahead to the good of future generations is something we seldom do in this era of instant gratification. Nowhere has this shortsightedness had a more devastating impact than on Mother Earth herself, the natural environment in which we live.

There has been some debate about the language of the biblical story of Adam and Eve. Some critics have attacked the idea that God gave Adam "dominion" over the earth. After all, "dominion" can easily become domination. But a closer look at the biblical account reveals that

Adam and Eve were entrusted with the stewardship of the earth; it was up to them to cultivate it and treat it properly, or they would have to live with the consequences.

What traditions like the Native American have done to balance the generally more arrogant European attitude is remind us that we cannot treat the natural world as if it were a mere commodity, or something we can possess in an absolute sense. We are indeed stewards, given an infinitely precious resource and charged with the responsibility of handing it on to our children without degradation.

One doesn't have to be an environmental activist to believe that we must care for the gloriously complex ecosphere that is our Earth. But unless everyone does something, however small or seemingly insignificant, we will all suffer in the long run.

⁂

And God said [to Adam and Eve]: Fill the earth and subdue it; and have dominion over the fish of the sea and over the birds of the air and over every living thing that moves upon the earth. . . . Behold, I have given you every plant yielding seed which is upon the face of all the earth, and every tree with seed in its fruit. . . . The Lord God took the man and put him in the Garden of Eden to till it and keep it.

Genesis 1:28–29, 2:15

The creeping things of the earth will give you lessons, and the fishes of the sea will tell you all.

Job 12:8

※

You shall not thus pollute the land in which you live.

Numbers 35:33

※

Not only one who cuts down food trees, but also one who [purposely and impulsively] smashes household goods, tears clothes, demolishes a building, stops up a spring, or destroys food violates the command, "You must not destroy" (Deuteronomy 20:19).

Maimonides

※

All art, all education, can be merely a supplement to nature.

Aristotle

※

Nature is not governed except by obeying her.

Francis Bacon

Nature is the art of God.

Dante

If you want to clear the stream, get the hog out of the spring.

American proverb

The earth was made for all, rich and poor, in common. Why do you rich claim it as your exclusive right?

St. Ambrose

Praised be You, my Lord, with all your creatures, especially Sir Brother Sun, who is the day and through whom you give us light. And he is beautiful and radiant with great splendors and bears likeness of You, Most High One.

St. Francis of Assisi

The slightest movement affects the whole of nature; one stone can alter the whole sea. Likewise, in the realm of grace, the slightest action affects everything because of its consequences; therefore everything matters. In every action we must look beyond the action at our present, past, and future state, and that of others affected by it, and see how all these things are connected. Then we shall exercise great restraint.

Blaise Pascal

Nature uses as little as possible of anything.

Johannes Kepler

Every part of this earth is sacred to my people. Every shining pine needle, every sandy shore, every mist in the dark woods, every clearing and humming insect is holy in the memory and experience of my people.

Chief Seattle of the Suquamish tribe

Each mortal thing does one thing and the same:
Deals out that being indoors each one dwells;
Selves—goes itself; myself it speaks and spells,
Crying What I do is me: for that I came.

Gerard Manley Hopkins

Love all God's creation, the whole and every grain of sand in it. Love every leaf, every ray of God's light. Love the animals, love the plants, love everything. If you love everything, you will perceive the divine mystery in things. Once you perceive it, you will begin to comprehend it every day. And you will come at last to love the whole world with an all-embracing love.

Fyodor Dostoyevsky

People have got to understand that the commandment, "Do unto others as you would that they should do unto you" applies to animals, plants and things, as well as to people! and that if it is regarded as applying only to people . . . then the animals, plants and things will, in one way or another, do as badly by man as man has done by them.

Aldous Huxley

The ground is holy, being even as it came from the Creator. Keep it, guard it, care for it, for it keeps men, guards men, cares for men. Destroy it and man is destroyed.

Alan Paton

In our every deliberation, we must consider the impact of our decisions on the next seven generations . . . on those faces that are yet beneath the ground.

The Great Law of the Six Nations Iroquois Confederacy

✳

This we know. The earth does not belong to man; man belongs to the earth. This we know. All things are connected. Whatever befalls the earth befalls the sons of the earth. Man did not weave the web of life. He is merely a strand in it. Whatever he does to the web, he does to himself.

Chief Seattle of the Suquamish tribe

✳

We abuse land because we regard it as a commodity belonging to us. When we see land as a community to which we belong, we may begin to use it with love and respect.

Aldo Leopold

✳

My boots crunched on the crust of snow but did not break through, and I pulled my hood up against the wet half-snow that fell as I started my February walk through the woodlot. I had been too long away. Subzero temperatures had kept me home and mostly indoors for nearly two months. At last I was out to see how my trees were faring, to see if the heavy snow and ice had broken them as they had broken the lawn trees in town, to see if widow makers waited in the treetops to end my labor on the ground. None did; my trees had fared well, and I walked easily, enjoying the radiance of the wet light under the leafless canopy. As I walked I grew more and more content, more and more at home, settled and pleased to be the caretaker of the wood I walked.

I grew up at the edge of a wood and in the midst of a large extended family. My grandparents, four aunts and uncles, and I don't know how many cousins and second cousins all lived along a dirt lane that bore our family name. The lane ran beside a small stream, turned up a steep hill through woods, and then cut sideways just below a cleared ridge that was usually planted in corn. Our house was on the low side of the road. A deep ravine sliced the edge of our backyard. A short path switched back and forth down its side into the second-growth hardwood that isolated us on our hill.

For the first seven years of my life those woods were my playground. My cousins and second cousins were my playmates. We were a scruffy bunch, born just before and just after the Second World War. I don't remember toys other than cap guns or dolls. But toys didn't matter, for we ranged in the woods like the untamed animals we were. It was a good life, full of lessons both moral and practical.

My task walking in the woodlot snow reminded me of a small incident. I must have been about six, for I was definitely a follower, bending to the influence of an uncle just a few years older than I was and to that of the cousins his age. They were allowed to roam farther afield than I was and knew deep places in the stream where one could swim. They carried hatchets and small axes in leather sheaths bought in the Boy Scout department in the large department store two towns away. These weapons were a crucial part of their equipment, necessary for "hacking," one of their favorite pastimes. Hacking involved running through the woods whacking great chunks of bark from the maples and oaks, leaving a small trail of white, bleeding blazes to mark a wanton passage. I begged my uncle to take me along. I wanted to hack my way through the woods the way he did.

But he looked at the rubber hatchet I brandished, and he laughed. "Get a real hatchet," he said, "and you can come."

When my father came home from work that afternoon, I asked for his hatchet, the one he used to chop the heads off the chickens I helped him slaughter. "What for?" he asked.

"I want to go hacking," I answered.

He returned me a puzzled look. "What is hacking?"

"Chopping trees," I replied.

"Are you building something?" he asked.

I began to sense something was wrong. "No," I answered, looking at my feet. "Hacking is just chopping trees."

"Whatever gave you that idea?" he asked.

"Uncle Butch," I answered. "He said I could go with him. Can I have the hatchet?"

"You don't chop trees for no reason," he said, and turned away.

I look off through the pattern of tree trunks rising before me. I am amazed that such a small incident has stayed with me, that it comes back so vividly after nearly fifty years. But more than that, I am amazed at my father's wisdom. He taught so lightly I did not know he was teaching. That day he shaped my conscience. Like Christ speaking a parable, he did not even explain. He spoke instead out of his character and placed in my mind an unshakable sense of the meaning of stewardship: the earth is not mine to use as I please.

I understand his words now, and as I walk, I echo them with words older than his: "The earth is the Lord's, and the fulness thereof."

THE OUTSTRETCHED
HAND: GIVING ALMS

An Islamic proverb says: "What I kept, I lost. What I spent, I had. What I gave, I have." Here, in a nutshell, is the accumulated wisdom of the ancients about the necessity of giving to the poor and needy. The old-fashioned term is "giving alms," the word alms being derived from the Greek word for "pity."

As with so many of the great moral precepts, the driving force behind the obligation to give to the poor is the recognition that they are essentially like us. How many of us can look upon the less fortunate without the thought crossing our minds, "There, but for the grace of God, go I"? Without this recognition of the dignity and humanity of the poor, the ancients remind us, our giving will be sterile and heartless. The spirit of the giver is as important as the gift itself.

But the types of gifts we can offer are indeed numerous. Writing a check and mailing it off and dropping coins in a cup are acts of generosity that are almost always praiseworthy. There are also times when money alone is not enough, when we can and should give food, tools, skills, understanding, and, above all, love. Moreover, the old proverbs ask us to start giving close to home. When we can look into the face of someone who is less fortunate, our giving will be more real, and more likely to be a permanent part of our character.

Open wide your hand to your brother, to the needy and to the poor.

Deuteronomy 15:11

The generous soul shall be enriched; and he who satisfies shall himself be satisfied.

Proverbs 11:25

Cast your bread upon the waters: for you shall find it after many days.

Ecclesiastes 11:1

Go and sell everything you have and give the money to the poor, and you will have treasure in heaven.

Matthew 19:21

Silver and gold have I none; but such as I have I give to thee.

Acts 3:6

It is more blessed to give than to receive.

Acts 20:35

Let everyone give as his heart tells him, neither grudgingly nor under compulsion, for God loves the man who gives cheerfully. After all, God can give you everything that you need, so that you may always have sufficient both for yourselves and for giving away to other people.

2 Corinthians 9:7–8

The question of bread for myself is a material question, but the question of bread for my neighbor is a spiritual question.

Nikolay Berdyayev

As a torch is not diminished though it kindles a million candles, so will not he lose who gives to a good cause.

Midrashim: Exodus Rabbah

If a poor man asks for alms, and you have nothing to give, console him with words; for it is forbidden to chastise a poor man or raise your voice against him, since his heart is broken.

Maimonides

The prayers of the poor are heard by God before the prayers of all others.

Zohar

The first perfection is: Giving. As a full jar overthrown pours out the liquid and keeps back nothing, even so shall your charity be without reserve—as a jar overturned.

From "The Ten Perfections," Sutta-Pitaka; Buddha-Vasma

The quickest generosity is the best.

Arab proverb

[Of a saintly woman]: Preferring to store her money in the stomachs of the needy rather than hide it in a purse.

St. Jerome

When people ask what they should spend in charity, say, "All that you have left over above your needs."

The Koran

If you give alms publicly, it is well; but it is better to give them secretly. Allah knows what you do.

The Koran

The angels asked: "O God, is there anything You have created stronger than rock?" God said: "Yes, iron is stronger than rock, for iron breaks it." The angels asked: "O Lord! Is there anything stronger than iron?" God said: "Yes, fire is stronger than iron; for fire melts it." The angels asked: "Is there anything stronger than fire?" God answered: "Yes, water is stronger than fire; for water extinguishes fire." The angels asked: "Is there anything stronger than water?" God said: "Yes, wind is stronger than water; for wind can put water into motion." Then the angels asked: "O Defender! Is there anything stronger than wind?" God said: "Yes, those who give charity and their left hand does not know what their right hand does, they overcome all."

Muhammad

He who loves with purity considers not the gift of the lover, but the love of the giver.

Thomas à Kempis

Better do a good deed near at home than go far away to burn incense.

Chinese proverb

Do all the good you can,
By all the means you can,
In all the ways you can,
In all the places you can,
To all the people you can,
As long as ever you can.

John Wesley

It is well to give when asked, but it is better to give unasked through understanding.

Kahlil Gibran

By Jove the stranger and the poor are sent,
And what to those is given, to Jove is lent.

Homer

Who gives to me teaches me to give.

Dutch proverb

Not what we give, but what we share—
For the gift without the giver is bare;
Who gives himself with his alms feeds three—
Himself, his hungering neighbor, and me.

James Russell Lowell

Let us not be satisfied with just giving money. Money is not enough, money can be got, but they need your hearts to love them. So, spread your love everywhere you go.

Mother Teresa

Complete possession is proved only by giving. All you are unable to give possesses you.

André Gide

꙳

It is possible to give without loving, but it is impossible to love without giving.

Richard Braunstein

꙳

My eldest daughter just turned seven and has started taking catechism classes in preparation for her First Holy Communion. A couple of weeks ago, she came up to me and asked whether Christ's injunction to give alms meant giving a blanket to an old man on a cold winter's night. I was astonished. "You can't possibly remember that," I said. "You were only eighteen months old."

After she had gone, I sat thinking of that night. It was January and bitterly cold. It was late and I was returning from visiting a friend. Rachel was bundled up in her snowsuit and I had spread a blanket over her car seat to keep her warm. She had fallen asleep. The car was old and the heating only worked when it felt like it, and that wasn't tonight. I remember praying, as we wound our way through empty streets, that we wouldn't break down in the middle of nowhere. How relieved I felt when I saw the lights of familiar landmarks.

I was thinking of how warm our house would be when I got home, and of my husband waiting anxiously at the door, when I saw a figure stumbling along in the middle of the road. I braked hard to avoid hitting him, went into a skid, and then ground to a juddering halt. Cursing more because the jolt of the car had wakened Rachel (she was a frustratingly light sleeper and I had been looking forward to carrying her straight from her car seat to her bed) than because we had been in any serious danger, I got out of the car, all set to give the man a piece of my mind.

It was then that I saw how old the man was and that he was wearing the most threadbare jacket I had ever seen. Instead of angry words, I found myself blurting out, "What do you think you're doing wandering about on a night like this?"—as if he were a child inappropriately dressed for the weather, and I were his mother. He just stared at me vacantly and mumbled something. I suddenly realized that he was dead drunk; I could smell the fumes from ten feet away.

I remember standing there looking at him while conflicting thoughts ran helter-skelter through my mind. On the one hand, he was obviously intoxicated, and any money I might give him would almost certainly be spent on drink. On the other, he was most certainly in need, and who was I to question how he spent the money? Then there was the fact that he was visibly shivering. I went over to him and took his hand. It felt like ice. And now I was closer I could actually hear his teeth chattering. It was that, I realized, that had made him speak so haltingly, not drunkenness alone. If he didn't get warm soon, he would surely die of cold. My mind was made up. "Wait here," I commanded. I went back to the car, where Rachel was bawling. "I need to borrow your blanket, sweetheart," I coaxed, stripping it off her. "To give to the cold man out there." At my words, she stopped crying and peered out of the window. I walked back to the man. "Here," I said, slinging the blanket around his shoulders and pressing into his hand all the money I had. It was only twenty bucks. He looked at me vacantly for a few moments; then his eyes seemed to clear. "God bless you," he said. Then, before I could offer to drive him to wherever he was going, he shambled off into the night.

When I got back into the car I found that I was trembling. Stories about angels appearing as men raced through my mind. Then I told myself that I was being foolish. He was just a drunk old man out on a cold night. That was all. Still, it was uncanny how quickly Rachel had stopped crying, as if she had understood something I hadn't. I glanced back in my rearview mirror. She was smiling and patting the place where her blanket had been. "Nice man," she kept saying. "Nice man." It was then that the words of Homer (which I had encountered in a college English class) leaped into my mind: "By Jove are the stranger and the poor sent, / And what to those is given, to Jove is lent."

After all those years, what I had forgotten, Rachel, with her childlike instinct for goodness, had remembered. It was enough to make me think.

※

I work in what is known as the nonprofit sector of the economy. I'd like to think that what I do makes a genuine contribution to the improvement of arts education in America. Indeed, I find the work to be deeply satisfying. But it isn't an easy life: funding for nonprofit organizations is notoriously difficult to come by, especially in the tough economic conditions of the last few years. Though I am paid about half what I could make in the private sector, I recently found myself struggling with my conscience about how much we as a family give to those who are less fortunate than ourselves. In my heart I knew that I was making too many excuses for not giving more. My work was idealistic, I reasoned; wasn't that a significant contribution to society? True, I could make do with fewer music CDs and other regular purchases, but surely I need not feel guilty about having a little pleasure in life. In my heart even I knew these weren't very persuasive arguments, but they served to put off any serious reckoning with the matter.

Then I came across a story that radically changed my whole way of looking at things. One morning, while reading the newspaper, I noticed a feature about someone known as the Money Man. Reading on, I learned that a sixty-nine-year-old retired postal clerk named Thomas

Cannon had just given a thousand-dollar check to a sailor from a Greek ship. The sailor was stranded in Newport News, Virginia, because the owners of the company that owned his ship had gone bankrupt and the sailor had no money to return home to his family. In itself, this act of generosity would be an amazing tribute to Mr. Cannon, but when I got to the end of the article I discovered that it was hardly an isolated incident in his life.

Mr. Cannon, it turned out, had given away nearly $85,000 over the last twenty-five years. For most of his life, he and his wife, Princetta, have lived in a small ramshackle house without central heating or air-conditioning in one of the poorest neighborhoods in Richmond, Virginia. He had ridden a bicycle to work for many years because cars were repeatedly vandalized along the streets where he lived. When he was forty-seven years old, he decided that he was not being generous enough and wrote a check for a thousand dollars to a local women's club to reward them for the work they were doing in a Richmond elementary school. "A message came in my consciousness," Cannon recalled, which told him to "Go upstairs, look in your [Bible]. I went upstairs and pulled out one of those at random. When I read it, I was astonished. It said, 'You did not choose Me, but I chose you, and appointed you, that you should go and bear fruit, and that your fruit should abide.'"

That was in 1972. In the intervening years, he has written many other thousand-dollar checks, though none of the recipients has ever asked him for money. He has even given away money to wealthy people. When asked about this, Cannon replied: "I felt I couldn't discriminate on the basis of income."

In 1990, Princetta had a stroke. Then, in 1994, she had a second stroke, which completely debilitated her. Ever since, Cannon has spent eighteen-hour days caring for Princetta. He sleeps in a sleeping bag by her bed in order to respond quickly if she has a bad dream or needs water. "I owe her this," he said. "We never had any quarrel over my giving money away. . . . Princetta's just never been a very materialistic person. If anything, she's more generous than I am."

News of the Money Man has now spread far and wide. He has won many humanitarian awards. Just recently, people from around the country sent money to buy the Cannons a new home. Cannon accepted this gift because, he said, it would help him to better care for Princetta. The cycle of his charity has now come full circle.

When I finished reading Thomas Cannon's story I knew that the time for excuses had ended. We are now making a more concerted effort to set aside money for the less fortunate, and we're finding that there is more of it than we could have imagined.

12

COMFORTING THE AFFLICTED

Why is it so hard for us to face sickness, handicaps, and other forms of physical and emotional suffering? Perhaps much of the difficulty has to do with fear. When we are confronted with pain, we feel guilty and uncomfortable, as if the person afflicted is from another planet, someone we can't relate to. The writer Flannery O'Connor, who suffered from and eventually died of the disease lupus, once wrote to a friend: "I have never been anywhere but sick." In a sense, affliction is a foreign country to which it is hard to travel.

Day after day we are bombarded with images of physical perfection and health that bear little resemblance to our own bodies or of those around us. Somehow we can trick ourselves into believing, if only for a moment, that this exercise machine or that drink will turn us into the bronzed gods and goddesses in the advertisements. But we avert our eyes from so much suffering.

The word "compassion," so central to the moral traditions, means "suffering with." Most of those who are ill in mind or body do not expect us to know exactly what their suffering is like. More often than not, they just want to be treated as human beings, and not aliens from another planet. Many people today who are suffering from diseases or other illnesses have found that their plight becomes much easier when they are able to see their life as a story that has meaning. The question we need to ask ourselves is: Will we be there to hear those stories?

✻

Beware of robbing a wretch, of attacking a cripple.

Amenemope

✻

I swear by Apollo Physician, by Asclepius, by Health, by Panacea, and by all the gods and goddesses, making them my witnesses, that I will carry out, according to my ability and judgment, this oath. . . . I will use treatment to help the sick according to my ability and judgment, but never with a view to injury and wrongdoing. I will keep pure and holy both my life and my art. . . . In whatsoever houses I enter, I will enter to help the sick, and I will abstain from all intentional wrongdoing and harm, especially from abusing the bodies of man or woman, bond or free. And whatsoever I shall see or hear in the course of my profession in my intercourse with men, if it be what should not be published abroad, I will never divulge, holding such things to be holy secrets. Now if I carry out this oath, and break it not, may I gain forever reputation among all men for my life and for my art; but if I transgress it and forswear myself, may the opposite befall me.

Hippocratic Oath

Rejoice with those who rejoice, weep with those who weep.

Romans 12:15

Whoever fails to visit a sick, friendless person is as if he shed his blood.

The Talmud

Give to the weary, visit the sick, support the poor.

Afrahat

The bread that you store up belongs to the hungry; the cloak that lies in your chest belongs to the naked; and the gold that you have hidden in the ground belongs to the poor.

St. Basil

The beauty of the soul shines out when a man bears with composure one heavy mischance after another, not because he does not feel them, but because he is a man of high and heroic temper.

Aristotle

Adversity doth best discover virtue.

Francis Bacon

Adversity is the state in which a man most easily becomes acquainted with himself.

Samuel Johnson

Bear ye one another's burdens.

Galatians 6:2

We commend to thy fatherly goodness all those who are any ways afflicted, or distressed, in mind, body, or estate.

The Book of Common Prayer

It often happens that the sicker man is the nurse to the sounder.

Henry David Thoreau

Lord, grant that I may seek to comfort rather than be comforted; to love rather than be loved.

Mother Teresa

I complained that I had no shoes, until I met a man who had no feet.

Benjamin Franklin

Before all things and above all things care must be taken of the sick, so that they may be served in very deed as Christ himself.

The Rule of St. Benedict

Dearest Lord, may I see you today and every day in the person of your sick, and, whilst nursing them, minister unto you. Though you hide yourself behind the unattractive disguise of the irritable, the exacting, the unreasonable, may I recognize you.

Mother Teresa

It's funny how names seem to stick in one's head even after many years have elapsed. I found myself thinking the other day about Mrs. Gowan. I first met her when I was a student in college and had volunteered to help in an elderly people's nursing home in my spare time. Mrs. Gowan (she never told me her first name) was blind; other than that and apart from a tendency to wander in her mind, she was in pretty good shape. But her family had gotten fed up with caring for her and had put her in a home. In a way, I could understand why. She was a very difficult person to deal with. She was furious with her family for abandoning her and had somehow gotten it into her head that the nurses and other patients were in a conspiracy with them. On top of that, she was from an aristocratic background and her manner was imperious, to put it mildly.

She was assigned to me in the afternoons so that the other patients in the home could get some peace from her interminable harangues. My task was to keep her in her room. "Just how am I to do that?" I remember asking the head nurse in desperation. "I'm sure you'll think of something," she said over her shoulder as her starched skirt crackled down the corridor.

I entered Mrs. Gowan's room with a sinking heart. She was sitting up in bed with a regal expression on her face. In addition, she had draped herself with as much of her family jewelry as she could get her hands on. The message was clear. She had donned her armor and was ready to do battle. The hours crawled by as she sat in stony silence, her eyes uncannily staring into mine while I nervously tried to make conversation. By the end of the afternoon I was exhausted and angry. I decided to fight fire with fire. The next day, I brought in a book and settled myself to read. "How dare you ignore me," she snapped. "You're being paid to entertain me." "Well, you're ignoring me," I retorted. "And for your information, I'm a volunteer, so I don't get paid." "Then why are you doing this?" she asked in a baffled tone.

I have thought long and hard over that question since. Why had I given up what precious spare time I had, to perform the thankless task of baby-sitting a crusty old woman? The only answer I can give is that that would be what my father would have wanted me to do. I remember him coming home from work exhausted, grabbing a quick bite to eat, then going out again to make his "rounds." He was a member of the St. Vincent de Paul Society, which tends to the sick and the elderly. He would trudge the streets of our hometown, knocking on doors and asking the old folks who lived there if they needed anything. Mostly they just wanted to talk, and he would sit patiently in their parlors while they poured out their woes. I remember asking him why he did it when he had come home particularly late one night. "'When I was sick, you visited me,'" he quoted. I never forgot his words, and when he was in his final illness, I moved back home so I could be near him.

As for Mrs. Gowan, we became friends, of a sort. She still treated me as if I were her servant, albeit a cherished one. We spent many happy hours together, with me reading Dickens aloud and her chatting about her great-grandchildren when she lost the thread of the story. I like to think that, in some small way, I helped make her happier in those few years I was working in the nursing home. I know my father would have thought so.

✳

I grew up in a loving family, and though I went through my share of adolescent rebellion, I emerged with a strong commitment to leading a moral life. However, while I was off at college, something happened that radically challenged my whole way of looking at the world. I began to receive phone calls from my parents telling me of problems my little brother was having in and out of school. He ran away from home several times and was often found wandering the streets of the big city we lived near. After a couple of years, my brother was finally diagnosed as suffering from a form of schizophrenia, and had to be cared for within an institution.

Though my heart went out to my brother, I found it very difficult to visit him. Most of the patients on his ward were in much worse condition than he—frequently screaming, babbling nonsense, or just huddled in a catatonic ball in some corner. I was frightened and repulsed by these stricken people, and I couldn't find a way to open myself to them. In a rather shallow fashion, I associated mental illness with the "abnormal" or the "deviant," much as past generations had locked up those who were considered "mad."

It was painful for me to witness the large mood swings my brother would go through, from affection to anger and resentment. He had always looked up to me, treating me as something of a god. Yet in his illness he often found ways to say the most wounding things. The strange thing was that despite his clouded mind, I would frequently see the sparks of his remarkable intelligence and charm. He became the favorite of nearly everyone who came in contact with him. Nevertheless, there were times when I could find nothing to say to him, and my visits became more infrequent.

But one day in church I found myself paying close attention to the reading of a passage in which Christ confronts those possessed by "demons." I'm no biblical scholar, but even then I realized that, however one interpreted passages such as this, it was clear that Jesus had great compassion for those whose minds were disturbed and distraught. He didn't blame them for evil behavior; he faced them calmly and brought healing love into their lives.

Slowly it dawned on me that for all my moral rectitude, I was lacking in compassion and courage. I made a new effort to see my brother more often, and to look into the faces of those with whom he lived. My smiles were often returned. I also gained a profound respect for the dedicated individuals who work with the mentally ill on a daily basis. And while my brother has not been miraculously cured, he now lives in his own apartment and holds down a part-time job. Though I've moved away, we talk frequently on the phone. I no longer think of these visits and phone calls as merely being kind to my brother; I know now that he has given me immeasurably more love and insight into the human heart than I ever could have imagined.

13

RESPECTING OUR ELDERS IN A YOUTH-ORIENTED CULTURE

Nowhere is the contrast between the world today and the traditional cultures of the past more apparent than in our treatment of the elderly. We live in a culture that worships youth so intensely that we have to speak of the old by using euphemisms such as "senior citizens." "Be young! Have fun!" advertisements instruct us. To be old is to be out of touch, a fuddy-duddy. The pressures of economics and modern "lifestyles"—some of which, admittedly, are beyond the control of many people—have broken apart the institution of the extended family, where the older generation lived in or near the home. And while there can be no doubt that "retirement homes" and other institutions for the elderly are necessary and humane places, most of us suspect that the old are too often looked upon as an unpleasant burden.

What a contrast this is to traditional cultures, which were unanimous in their respect for the wisdom and insights possessed by the elders of the community. In the modern era there has been such a bias in favor of "progress" that we tend to think of the young as being more advanced, more "with it." Traditional cultures, however, were much more skeptical about the amount of progress any one generation can make. Most of the truths we possess, the sages argued, remain the same from one generation to the next. The key is whether anyone can acquire an understanding of these truths over the course of a lifetime of experience and moral insight.

We pride ourselves today on being more enlightened and less prejudiced than in the past, but if we were honest we would admit that we have our own set of biases. While our families and neighborhoods crumble around us, perhaps it is time that we gather the older members of our community around us, and begin to learn some of the truths we are in danger of forgetting.

There is no happiness where there is no wisdom;
No wisdom but in submission to the gods.
Big words are always punished,
And proud men in old age learn to be wise.

Sophocles

Ask your father and he will tell you, your elders and they shall instruct you.

Deuteronomy 32:7

Rise up before the hoary head, and honor the face of an old man.

Leviticus 24:22

Do not dishonor the old: we shall all be numbered among them.

Ecclesiasticus 8:7

Cast me not off in the time of old age; forsake me not when my strength faileth.

Psalms 71:9

Rebuke not an elder, but entreat him as a father.

1 Timothy 5:1

A youth, when at home, should be filial, and, abroad, respectful to his elders.

Confucius

The prosperity of a country can be seen simply in how it treats its old people.

Nahman of Bratslav

Age is not all decay; it is the ripening, the swelling, of the fresh life within, that withers and bursts the husk.

George MacDonald

One of the many pleasures of old age is giving things up.

Malcolm Muggeridge

Let your old age be childlike, and your childhood like old age; that is, so that neither may your wisdom be with pride, nor your humility without wisdom.

St. Augustine

A man is not old and venerable because gray hairs are on his head. If a man is old only in years he is indeed old in vain.

The Dhammapada

To honor an old man is to show respect for God.

Muhammad

To grow old is to grow from passion to compassion.

Albert Camus

Old age
level light
evening in the afternoon
love without the bitterness and so
good-night

Archibald MacLeish

I mailed the house payment each month to Mr. and Mrs. Fathers, the elderly couple who had sold it to us. After Mr. Fathers died, Mrs. Fathers moved to an assisted-living facility nearby.

When my husband was laid off, we were barely able to scrape together the funds for the house payment until just before the month's end. I wanted to get the check into Mrs. Fathers's hands right away, so I bundled my young son into the stroller and walked the two blocks to the facility where Mrs. Fathers lived.

We entered her room to find a world constructed with the same meticulous care as the home we had bought from them. I recognized some of the beautiful antiques, and the intricate bedspread she had crocheted. Framed needlework decorated the walls. I knew the sheets in her closet were ironed and folded in the perfect linen towers that had impressed me during our house hunt.

She greeted us with a gracious reserve that lasted only until my toddler engaged her attention. She catered to his every need, offering toys, snacks, anything to form a bond. She was so taken with my son that she forgot all about me. To overcome my awkwardness, I started asking questions. Things like: "How are you?" "Do you get many visitors?"

Gradually it came out that she had no family to care for her. Because of her deteriorating vision, she needed some basic assistance: rides to the dentist and doctor, an occasional shopping trip, and so on. If she couldn't get help she would have to move to a nursing care facility where she would be required to shed the last of the beautiful vestiges of her home.

I mentally reviewed the reasons I couldn't help her: my own family needed me; I was involved in church activities; I had no time. Still, I felt compelled to respond. I kept thinking about the verse: "Pure religion . . . is this: to visit the fatherless and widows in their affliction."

I reluctantly chose to follow those words. From that point on, I hand-delivered the house payment each month so I could check on how Mrs. Fathers was getting on. I told her to call me if she was *really* stuck for a ride. And call she did. Frequently. Our interactions weren't exactly comfortable, but I knew that she was grateful and that I was doing the right thing.

Even after we moved, I continued to visit Mrs. Fathers when she needed me. Then one day, someone from her church phoned me to let me know she had passed away. Saddened by her death, I realized that we had gotten into a natural rhythm: she had a need and I would duly respond. I had no way of knowing how great a need the relationship would meet later in my own life.

Several years after Mrs. Fathers died, my finances were at the lowest they had ever been. We were barely surviving from month to month. After sixteen years of spending my days at home with my children, I had to get a paying job with health benefits. I responded to an ad in the paper for an activities director at an assisted-care facility. I remembered my interaction with Mrs. Fathers, and knew my creative skills would combine with that to make me a possible candidate.

During the course of my conversation with the director, she asked a strange question: "Do you have any aversion to working with seniors?"

I thought about Mrs. Fathers and what she had taught me. I knew what the elderly residents would need from me. They needed to be talked with as adults. They were hard of hearing, not stupid. They needed a friend, not another distant clinician. They were fragile, having endured the most devastating blow a person can experience: the loss of their home and their independence. They needed help to maintain their dignity and as much control of their lives as possible.

"No," I said with confidence. "I have no aversion to working with seniors."

I got the job. It's a great job. Many people fear aging and death, so they don't want to relate to older adults, but I've found that elderly people have time to spend building relationships. Most seniors notice what I do for them and are quick to thank me for even the smallest kindness.

Life is a circle. Give and you shall receive, pressed down, shaken together in good measure. I'm not sure who's getting more.

In My End Is My Beginning: The Meaning of Death

It has been said—and we think truly—that death is the dirty little secret of the modern era. It seems that we will go to almost any length to look away from this fundamental truth about our existence. Hospitals and retirement homes often make death clinical and remote from our immediate experience; cemeteries are given bland and innocuous names like Forest Lawn. Above all, there is the simple fact that, as a society, we simply avoid the subject of death. At times, the silence can be deafening.

In contrast, the moral sensibilities of the past were founded on an honest recognition of our mortality. To the thinkers of the past the meaning of death was that it is an essential part of life, that it was the natural conclusion of the story of our lives. It is important to remember that in these traditions the idea of an afterlife did not cheapen the value of our worldly existence. To Greek philosophers such as Plato, it was only at the moment of death that one could see the completed story, the fulfillment of a life well lived. Even the religious traditions stressed that our lives on earth were a profoundly meaningful gift, a training ground for the soul.

Human beings have always reacted to death with anger and fear— emotions that are natural and understandable. But those who have attempted to ignore death have inevitably fallen into either arrogance or despair. The sages and philosophers remind us that without death our actions become arbitrary. Death makes us accountable, asks us to choose wisely so that those who come after us have a better life. Once we accept our mortality we can perceive the meanings that transcend it. "Love is as strong as death," says the Song of Solomon. If we live our lives well, "Ripeness is all."

Remember: it is not given to man to take his goods with him. No one goes away and then comes back.

From the tomb of King Inyotef of Egypt, 2600 B.C.

Love is as strong as death.

Song of Solomon 8:6

Yea, though I walk through the valley of the shadow of death, I will fear no evil: for thou art with me.

Psalms 23:4

In a harbor, two ships sailed: one setting forth on a voyage, the other coming home to port. Everyone cheered the ship going out, but the ship sailing in was scarcely noticed. To this, a wise man said: "Do not rejoice over a ship setting out to sea, for you cannot know what terrible storms it may encounter and what fearful dangers it may have to endure. Rejoice rather over the ship that has safely reached port and brings its passengers home in peace."

And this is the way of the world: When a child is born, all rejoice; when someone dies, all weep. We should do the opposite. For no one can tell what trials and travails await a newborn child; but when a mortal dies in peace, we should rejoice, for he has completed a long journey, and there is no greater boon than to leave this world with the imperishable crown of a good name.

The Talmud

Fear not that your life shall come to an end, but rather that it shall never have a beginning.

John Henry Newman

So, my judges, face death with a good hope, and know for certain that no evil can happen to a good man, either in life or after death.

Socrates

Death be not proud, though some have called thee
Mighty and dreadful, for thou art not so,
For those whom thou think'st thou dost overthrow,
Die not, poor death, nor yet canst thou kill me. . . .
One short sleep past, we wake eternally,
And death shall be no more; death, thou shalt die.

John Donne

Life is a state of embryo, a preparation for life. A man is not completely born until he has passed through death.

Benjamin Franklin

O death, where is thy sting? O grave, where is thy victory?

1 Corinthians 15:55

If I err in my belief that the souls of men are immortal, I gladly err, nor do I wish this error, in which I find delight, to be wrested from me.

Cicero

This life is only a prelude to eternity. For that which we call death is but a pause, in truth a progress into life.

Seneca

We shall all be changed, in a moment, in the twinkling of an eye.

1 Corinthians 15:51–52

I shall hear in Heaven.

Ludwig van Beethoven

Death is the supreme festival on the road to freedom.

Dietrich Bonhoeffer

Men must endure
Their going hence, even as their coming hither:
Ripeness is all.

William Shakespeare

✳

As a well-spent day brings happy sleep, so life well used brings happy death.

Leonardo da Vinci

✳

Our theories of the eternal are as valuable as are those which a chick which had not broken its way through its shell might form of the outside world.

The Buddha

✳

From the unreal lead me to the real
From darkness lead me to light
From death lead me to immortality.

The Upanishads

My bags are packed and I am ready to go.

Pope John XXIII

⁕

To renounce all is to gain all; to descend is to rise; to die is to live.

Karl Rahner

⁕

Eternal rest grant unto them, O Lord; and let perpetual light shine upon them.

Roman Missal

⁕

No man should be held responsible for the words he utters in his grief.

The Talmud

⁕

While I was growing up, my mother, Bess, often spoke of an old friend whom she'd loved very much. I only came to understand the depth of their relationship much later in life, when it transcended time and space in a small but beautiful gesture.

Bess was born into a family marked by sadness. It wasn't spoken about or acknowledged; in many ways it was overcome. Still, there was melancholy underneath, and a sense of bitterness among the small group of four: father, mother, older brother, and Bess. Her father was popular, dazzling, successful; her mother beautiful and demure; her brother, everyone's favorite, hero and golden boy. But the father lived a wild life; the mother resented his ways, turned inward, and became distant; the son took out his frustration at the unspoken despair of his parents—who loved each other, but didn't know how to go about it—by becoming a behavior problem. Bess, who was not so much ignored as forgotten, was saddest of all.

But something happened in Bess's life to make the sadness bearable—a gift which showed her that joy, too, was a possibility in life. When Bess was born, one of the nurses who assisted in the delivery took note of the problems that were haunting Bess's family. The nurse, whose name was Dee Dee, had no family of her own; she decided to become a friend to the child. It happened that Dee Dee lived in the large boardinghouse owned by Bess's grandmother. Since this was during the Depression, Bess's family also lived in the same house. This gave Dee Dee the opportunity to see her decision come to flower.

"Why'd you pick me, Dee Dee?" Bess often asked, perplexed, "of all the children you delivered? Why'd you pick me?"

Dee Dee shrugged and gave what seemed a satisfactory answer, a true answer: "Oh, you looked liked you needed somebody to love you. And I needed somebody to love."

Throughout her childhood, Bess spent her weekends with Dee Dee, who took her to all the places an old woman takes a young girl: to the park, to the zoo, to stores, to church most of all: and to some places it is rare for a child to be taken by anyone, no matter who is her guide: the beaches of the Gulf Coast, the boroughs of New York, the city of Boston. Dee Dee was a constant source of good in the girl's life, and saw her through painful times, such as her brother's tragic death and her parents' remorse and deepening sorrow. Bess and Dee Dee's friendship lasted throughout the girl's adolescence, and even into her years away at college. Though Dee Dee's health was failing, Bess often came home to see her. The old woman died just before the girl graduated. Bess came home for the funeral, but after a few months she married and moved far away.

Years passed. Bess's parents grew old and moved to be closer to their only living child. Her life was busy with work and a husband and children of her own. She rarely had a chance to go back to her hometown, and when she did, it was not for long. One day, however, after her children had grown and her parents had passed away, she and her husband had more time to spend in the town. She resolved to visit her old friend's grave. Her memory foggy, she inquired of an acquaintance, whose family had been in charge of the funeral, where the grave might be. To her shock, though the woman could name the cemetery, she was not certain where the grave was located.

"I'm not sure if anybody ever had a gravestone put up for her," said the woman. "I don't know who would've been responsible for that. Her family, of course. But then, she had none."

When Bess and her husband got to the cemetery, she had the groundskeeper locate the grave. Dee Dee was indeed buried there—the man knew the exact spot—but, as Bess feared, the grave had never been marked.

"That's something family usually does," the man said.

Bess nodded, agreeing; "I'm family," was her reply.

Before she left town, she bought a gravestone, gave instructions for the inscription, and ensured that it would be installed at the earliest possible time. All of this occurred some thirty-five years after Dee Dee's death.

An old monk was once asked why he cared for ancient graves, and why he cleaned the stones to preserve the writings carved there. His reply was simple: "They still have their names. They will always have their names."

A life infused with love has consequences that reach beyond time—ensuring that names, and places, and memories of what was still are, and always will be. They are not dead, can never die.

FOR OUR
CHILDREN'S
CHILDREN: WORKING
FOR POSTERITY

The actions we take have often been compared to stones dropped in a pond. The ripples that move outward from the point of impact can be felt from a great distance away. So it is with our moral lives. Choices made today will affect our children and our children's children. When we forget this fact, and act only for the moment, we play a dangerous game with the future.

The statesman Edmund Burke once spoke of the "great mysterious incorporation of the human race" linking past, present, and future generations. If the opposite of selfishness is thinking of others, then a generous definition of "others" must include those who come after us.

Thus we come full circle, back to the most fundamental of all relationships, that between the parent and the child. When children look into our eyes, their look is full of trust and confidence. The rest is up to us.

. . . visiting the iniquity of the fathers upon the children, and upon the children's children, unto the third and fourth generation.

Exodus 34:7

There are three things which are unfilial, and to have no posterity is the greatest of them.

Mencius

People will not look forward to posterity, who never look backward to their ancestors.

Edmund Burke

Man's fate is his character.

Heraclitus

What we look for does not come to pass. God finds a way for what none foresaw.

Euripides

Most men prefer and strive for the present, we for the future.

St. Ambrose

Every oak was once an acorn.

Elmer Wheeler

When we are planning for posterity, we ought to remember that virtue is not hereditary.

Thomas Paine

The most effective way to confront the future is to confront the present courageously and constructively.

Rollo May

Hope to the end.

1 Peter 1:13

One of my enduring memories from childhood is sitting on my grandfather's knee with a big children's Bible spread out before us. I was barely older than two when he started reading to me every night after he got home from work. It became one of our most cherished rituals, and I can still recall, after all these years, the picture of Daniel in the lion's den, and of the three holy boys in the fiery furnace with their hands joined in prayer and their faces lifted ecstatically toward heaven.

I was so devoted to these nightly readings, my grandmother told me, that I would stand at the garden gate each evening with the Bible in my hands, waiting for the first glimpse of my grandfather. Of course, when I was a young child, it never occurred to me that Grampa would be tired after his day's work and would prefer to sit down and rest when he got home. He worked for a newspaper, and in those days before the printing business was run by computers, he would stand for hours setting type. But he never showed any signs of impatience when I would run down the road to greet him, lugging the Bible in my arms. We would walk back to the house hand in hand; he would take off his coat and then settle me on his lap and open those magical pages.

At the age of three, I astonished him by pointing to the beginning of a story and carefully reading the opening paragraph. I still recall the word that gave me the most trouble—"Nebuchadnezzar." At first Grampa couldn't believe that I was actually reading at the age of three. I remember him turning to another page and pointing to a passage at random; he was amazed when I duly read it off more or less correctly. That was the beginning of my enchantment with books, which has stayed with me all my life.

But it is not only my precocious reading ability that I attribute to my grandfather. Somehow, during those moments we shared poring over the Bible, he instilled in me a love of stories. Not a literary man, he was nevertheless a devoted Christian who believed that everyone ought to be as familiar with the stories of the Old Testament as they were with the New Testament. He himself had read the Bible in its entirety twice in his life.

As I grew older, my love of stories likewise grew, and I decided that I wanted to become a writer. One of the greatest sorrows in my life is that my grandfather never saw me graduate from college; he himself had left school at thirteen. (My brother and I were the first generation in our family to attend college.) Nor was I ever able to send him the books that I published in later life. But what comforts me is the knowledge that, if it weren't for him, I would have become neither a university graduate nor a writer. During those hours we spent together he unwittingly planted the seeds of what I would become, and of what would be one of my chief joys in life. I like to think that, wherever he is, he would be proud of my achievement and smile at his part in it.